Give Me Jesus

SINGING, PRAYING & CELEBRATING OUR LIFE IN CHRIST

G-7501

Give Me Jesus

Singing, Praying & Celebrating Our Life in Christ

Reflections & Prayers

David Haas

Also available:

Double Compact Disc • CD-803

Music Collection • G-7502

GIA Publications, Inc
Chicago

Edited by Tom Backen
Cover Design: Martha Chlipala
Book Design: Robert Sacha

G-7501
Copyright © 2009 GIA Publications, Inc.
7404 South Mason Avenue, Chicago, Illinois 60638

Printed in the United States of America

ISBN: 978-1-57999-754-0

Other Books by David Haas Available from GIA Publications:

With Every Note I Sing • G-4392

I Will Sing Forever • G-5649

With You by My Side, Volume One: The Journey of Life • G-5785

With You by My Side, Volume Two: Confirmation • G-5786

To Worship in Spirit and Truth • G-6521

The Biblical Way of the Cross • G-6615

A Time to Pray: With the Old Testament • G-6722

A Time to Pray: With the New Testament • G-6654

A Time to Pray: For Justice and Peace • G-6868

The Holy Presence of God • G-7154

To Give You a Future with Hope • G-7153

Contents

Contents

In Gratitude

While it is impossible to celebrate individually all of the wonderful friends and saints who grace and shape my life and who have influenced this project, I feel compelled to offer some specific thanks. I first want to thank Alec Harris, Michael Cymbala, Kelly Dobbs Mickus, Tom Hawley, Andrew Schultz and everyone at GIA Publications for their ongoing and tireless support of my creative and pastoral work. I am grateful to Fr. Michael Joncas, Sr. Roberta Kolasa, SJ, Art Zannoni and Sr. Gertrude Foley, SC for being such wonderful friends, mentors and teachers. I also give thanks to Lori True for her friendship, loving support, creativity, passion for ministry, and for always offering honesty and valued critique.

I want to express my gratitude to my colleagues at Benilde-St. Margaret's High School in St. Louis Park, Minnesota, especially Tom Backen for his generosity and skill in editing my words, to Holly Hoey Germann for her helpful comments and to Joel Loecken, Maura Brew, Becca Walsh, Dr. Sue Cipolle, May Lane Bernardo, Dr. Bob Tift, Sr. Jeanne Marie Vanderlinde, OSB, Paul Keefe and Dr. Sue Skinner. Thanks go out to Leisa Anslinger for her suggestions and to Bill Huebsch for his vision of catechesis that always inspires my thinking. I am also very appreciative to Gregg Sewell for his work copy editing the final manuscript, to Fr. Ron Krisman for his review of the text and to Steve Wiese and Miles Hanson at Creation Audio in Minneapolis for their help in the final engineering, sequencing and mastering of the CD recording.

I want to give thanks to dear friends Kate Cuddy, Rob and Mary Glover and their family, Tom Franzak, Matt Reichert, Fr. Ray East, Mary Werner, Joe Camacho, Fr. George DeCosta, Bonnie Faber, Tim Westerhaus, Steve Kron, Fr. Joe Kempf, Kathy and Glenn Baybayan, George Miller, Eileen Bird, Fr. Alapaki Kim, Paul Tate, Rob Strusinski, Sr. Bridget Waldorf, SSND, Zack Stachowski, Br. Dennis Schmitz, SM, Stephen Petrunak, Bobby Fisher, Barbara Conley-Waldmilller, Jim Waldo Jo Infante, Jesse Manibusan, Eileen Frischmon, David Dreher, Paulette Ching and to the entire Music Ministry Alive! community. I am always thankful to my parents and to Jeffrey, Colleen and Helen.

Finally, to Sr. Kathleen Storms, SSND, for her insights, guidance and wisdom that not only fed and influenced much of what may be found in these pages, but also what has been shared so lavishly with me in the midst of the many interesting turns of my spiritual journey. It is to her that this project is dedicated.

Introduction

The Gospel courageously celebrates and proclaims boldly that Jesus Christ is alive. This living presence is more than just a memory for those who follow his teaching, for he, his very self, lives. This Jesus who walked the earth, the one who taught, performed miracles, and prophetically proclaimed the Reign of God, was raised from the dead after a cruel execution. But the story does not end there. The Spirit of Jesus was given to breathe and dwell among all who would believe and surrender their lives in discipleship, affirming the awesome truth that Jesus lives and moves beyond a single time in history. We are called to be vessels of the Risen One, to become the living presence of Christ to one another and to the world. The simple truth is that this presence can truly transform all of creation.

How is this presence received? We freely choose it, in response to Christ's gracious invitation. Christ does not manipulate or coerce us, but he does wait for our consent, for our "yes." We who have had an authentic experience of Jesus often find it difficult or impossible to describe, as it exists outside the bounds of normal understanding. It is deeply spiritual and often filled with mystery. The presence of Christ is more about *his being known* than our knowing. It is more about *his being apprehended* than our apprehending. It cannot be forced, for it is pure gift. The story of this Christ has been and is continually shared through the many voices and perspectives of mystics, saints, philosophers, theologians, poets, composers, sculptors, preachers, painters, musicians, and dancers; the educated and uneducated; the rich and poor. Sometimes the story is experienced in visions or dreams, sometimes it is very dramatic, and sometimes it is found in stillness and calm, in the most ordinary things of life.

For Christians, the celebration of the liturgy is the central event in which we recognize this presence, in which we are called to pray, sing, lament, and to praise God through the offering of our lives and service to Jesus Christ. Because the liturgy is *sung*, liturgical music is the language believers use to join in the great paschal song of praise for the victory of life over death. The life, death, and resurrection of Christ—this is the praise we sing and the gift that thrusts us forward into a life of discipleship. Through, with, and in faith we sing this song; we reach out in solidarity with other members of the Christian tribe to deepen our relationship and our life of discipleship with the Risen Jesus, given for the life of the world.

While the liturgy is the heartbeat of the life of the Church, and while music helps the blood flow in and through the ritual event, liturgy and its music are not the actual *heart* of Christianity itself. Jesus was not primarily concerned with liturgy, and certainly not with music. The Gospels contain no sermon or parable that addresses the topic of music. Jesus did, however, proclaim the Reign of God, and he calls each and every one of us to be servants of this mission and cause. As lovers, ministers, and participants in the prayer of liturgical music, our primary charge is to deepen our commitment to Christ and to make that same Christ known and proclaimed to the world.

Before it is anything else, the ministry of liturgical music is our communal (and also, at times, personal) language for singing, praying, and celebrating our lives in Christ. The unique language of music can proclaim what mere spoken words and doctrines cannot accomplish adequately: the celebration and wonder of the profound presence of Christ and the liberation found in the Reign of God. One of the most important qualities of liturgical music is that it is *participatory*. The sacred melodies, sounds and rhythms of our sung prayer empower the gathered assembly to give "full, conscious, and active participation" in, yes, liturgical celebration, but *also* in and through the witness of our lives.[1] This being the case, while our sung prayer is liturgical, it is also catechetical and formational. But it is catechetical in ways far beyond our usual understanding of catechesis, as revealed to us in *The General Directory for Catechesis* (GDC), so beautifully paraphrased by Bill Huebsch:

> Down through the ages, God has revealed himself to us,
> culminating in Christ,
> who completed and perfected Revelation.
>
> Jesus Christ is God's own Son,
> > the final event among all the events of salvation history.
> > Catechesis begins here:
> > it must show who Jesus Christ is,
> > his life and ministry,
> > and present Christian faith as the following of Christ.[2]

I cannot imagine a better job description or role definition for the ministry of liturgical music, which includes not only those who are charged with the leadership of sung prayer, but *all of God's people* who sing it, pray it, and search for the grace to live it. Liturgical music is set forth to give voice to "who Jesus Christ is," and to do so with passion and fidelity. Music in our liturgical worship has the power to deepen our participation and shape what we believe, engaging this participation in faith at the liturgy in ways that no other liturgical art can accomplish. At the same time, musical sung prayer hopefully strengthens how we witness the Christian life beyond the liturgical celebration itself.

Think about how often certain liturgical songs have been able to endure and nurture the hearts of worshippers after the liturgy is over. Could we name anyone who could *recite* totally by heart the words to Psalm 91? Then think again as to how many can sing by heart all of the words to *On Eagle's Wings* (a musical setting of Psalm 91).[3] Now compare how many people remember and continue to whistle or hum a song prayed at Mass as opposed to remembering the message of a particular homily. For many, liturgical music has been a primary teacher and source of scripture, a vital expression of their faith. The attributes of melody, rhythm, harmonic structure, and phrasing can cut through the surface and communicate the message in a unique way that touches the heart, and often, transforms lives. Music, and the particular ministry of liturgical music, *can be that powerful.*

The GDC continues in setting forth the challenge of our mission as a praying and singing Church:

> Indeed, the very purpose of the Church
> is to evangelize.
> There are various aspects of this, which are all connected.
> First there is the call to proclaim,
> > then to make disciples and teach,
> > then to witness to Christ personally,
> > then to baptize,
> > then to do this in memory of Christ,
> > and finally, to love one another in the process.
>
> These are the means by which the Gospel is passed on,
> the means, in other words,
> of evangelization.[4]

Therefore, the role of liturgical music is—in its composition, in its "performance" in liturgy, and how it compels us to act and serve after the liturgical event—also a ministry of *evangelization*, which awakens and strengthens faith. Liturgical music is an artistic medium that assists the Church to make disciples, to teach, witness, keep the memory of Jesus and our baptism alive, and to love and care for one another through every step of the journey. Our music, our texts, all of our vocal and instrumental utterances—they all flow from this source. Our songs of faith, praise, and lament are to be expressions and agents of conversion:

> In Mark 1:15, Jesus calls us
> to "repent and believe the good news."
> Today we speak of this as "conversion and faith";
> > evangelization invites us to both.

Conversion is first. It is the first and sincere
    adherence to the person of Christ
    and the decision to walk in his footsteps.
Faith is a personal encounter with Jesus Christ,
    making oneself a disciple,
    and it demands a permanent commitment
    to think, judge, and live like him.
Toward this end, the believer is united
    to the community of disciples
    and takes on the faith of the Church.[5]

Liturgical music, then, is a musical and a singularly unique method of communication and storytelling that can nurture conversion, transformation, and discipleship. Obviously, its primary vocation is to serve the prayer and action of the liturgy, but its grace can reach far beyond the confines of the sacred space of a church, chapel, or oratory. Liturgical music can find a home beyond the liturgy in the midst of catechetical events, retreats, sacred music concerts, and also in our personal life of prayer and spiritual growth. Its unique expression can serve the heart of evangelization and should also help provoke all to be attentive to the social mission of the Church, as our bishops aptly instruct us:

> Charity, justice and evangelization are thus the normal consequences of liturgical celebration. Particularly inspired by sung participation, the body of the Word Incarnate goes forth to spread the Gospel with full force and compassion.[6]

These are not soft words leaving room for negotiation. The normal consequences of our participation in sung prayer should be missionary, calling forth from us a committed and total life-response of justice-making and discipleship. We do this by singing and introducing the community to "who Jesus Christ is." Our musical prayer, both in our repertoire choices and in our presentation, should help make this Christ known, loved, celebrated, honored, and *sung* by and through the building of the Reign of God that he so passionately preached.

For some of us, music is already a preferred method and expression in our prayer life. Others of us have difficulty with this form of prayer, not because of a poverty of belief but because we may feel inadequate or deficient musically. For others, they feel that there is no melody in their heart, which points to a poverty of the *spiritual*. All of us *can* and *need* to sing our common prayer, both our praise and our lament, even if we think the sound may not seem pleasant to others. St. James would have us move beyond our self-consciousness and isolation: "Are any among you suffering? They should pray. Are any cheerful? They should sing songs of praise."[7]

In liturgy or any other gathering of communal prayer, or even in the solitude of our personal prayer time, music is and can be, a spiritual practice to help us engage in a holy conversation with Christ, inviting us to celebrate this presence in a beautiful, human way. All of us, both the musically trained and untrained, enter into the conversation equally, for musical skill is not the issue—the issue is that all of us, each in our own way, are called to enter into the song.

What are the unique characteristics of such a spiritual practice of sung prayer? In the context of the liturgical celebration itself there are, of course, the musical, technical, and aesthetic attributes as to what makes "good" music. This requires skill, craft, and reverence for beauty. There are also the critical liturgical and participatory considerations with attentiveness to ritual action as well as careful attention to texts that authentically articulate a healthy theology of our tradition. These are essential prerequisites. But in Christian liturgical music the key source and target of all of these energies in and beyond liturgy is to sing and proclaim, however clumsily, the person of Jesus: his life, his death, his resurrection, and his passionate and intimate activity in our lives. This cause begins in our liturgical prayer, but it should never end there:

> The paschal hymn, of course, does not cease when a liturgical celebration ends. Christ, whose praises we have sung, remains with us and leads us through church doors to the whole world, with its joys and hopes, griefs and anxieties.[8]

In *Give Me Jesus*, I hope to contribute to this spiritual practice by presenting a musical journey that invites us to sing, pray, and celebrate our lives in Christ. Here I have chosen forty-four liturgical song-prayers that I have composed, recorded, and published over the past twenty-six years that focus on different aspects of the person, mission, and redemptive story of Jesus. This book and the accompanying CD (CD-803) are offered as a gift for all who may not only sing and pray this music at liturgy but who also find such music a vehicle for their personal prayer and spiritual growth.

The songs and reflections provided are opportunities for *mystagogia*: to "break open" the mystery of Jesus Christ. Just as in the honored practice and tradition of *lectio divina*, in which we meditate and pray upon a scripture passage that is proclaimed or read, here the primary *"lectio"* is the music, the actual song-prayer itself. Both the text of the song (which is sometimes biblical, but not always), and the musical enshrinement of the words should be considered.

As you listen to the CD and pray along with this book you will see the music and text on the left-hand page and, on the facing right-hand page, a "breaking open" of the message followed by reflection questions and a concluding prayer. These can be utilized in your private prayer, as well as in group settings such as retreats, bible study groups, adult or youth catechetical events, and formation experiences for choirs, cantors, and other ministers of music, as well as other gatherings intended for reflection and spiritual growth. Feel free to adapt and be creative as to how these reflections can be used along with the recorded music.

The texts of these songs and hymns come from many sources. Included here are musical settings of biblical texts from the Gospels and letters of the New Testament. There are also pieces that find their inspiration from biblical texts that move beyond and explore new images. In addition, there are songs from the insights of saints and heroes and the African-American spiritual tradition; others are musical settings of texts written by contemporary text writers, and some are my own original texts. Some of these pieces have found their way into the repertoire of many parishes and other communities of faith over the years, and others may be new or more unfamiliar.

I hold no arrogance or illusion that these selections provide a complete presentation of the life, teaching and redemption given to us in Jesus the Christ. These musical prayers humbly express and celebrate a glance into the person and mission of Jesus. In compiling this collection I have come to remember the many pastoral settings, life-events, and stories that gave life to these songs. Originally composed for the liturgy, they represent my own musical and pastoral attempts to present different images, aspects, and explorations of the Christ that I have come to know in my experience of the liturgical and spiritual life of the Church and in the midst of my own conversion journey.

It is my deepest hope that all who listen, sing, pray, and reflect upon these liturgical songs will find a spiritual practice and lens in which to see and know more deeply the Jesus that many believers have come to discover, know, celebrate, and wrestle with. This Jesus offers an invitation to all of us to engage in the amazing song of faith, hope, love, and the promise of new life, leading us to embrace the Gospel of justice, mercy, and compassion. May these song-prayers help us all to rise above ourselves and engage in a spiritual conversation, "meeting Jesus again for the first time."[9] This conversation cannot be one-sided; we are called to respond in a dialogue of faith with the one who knows us well, and who calls us by name. And what is our response? Give me Jesus.

David Haas
11 January 2009
The Baptism of the Lord

Notes

1. Second Vatican Council, Constitution on the Sacred Liturgy (*Sacrosanctam Concilium*) (SC), n.14 in Vatican Council II: *Constitutions, Decrees, Declarations* (rev. trans. in inclusive language), edited by Austin Flannery (Northport, NY: Costello Publishing, 1996).
2. Bill Huebsch, *The General Directory for Catechesis in Plain English* (Twenty-Third Publications, 2001) n.40–41.
3. Michael Joncas, *On Eagle's Wings* (Oregon Catholic Press, 1979).
4. Huebsch, n.46.
5. Ibid, n.53.
6. United States Conference of Catholic Bishops, *Sing to the Lord: Music in Divine Worship* (USCCB Publishing, 2008), n.9.
7. James 5:13.
8. United States Conference of Catholic Bishops, n.8.
9. Marcus J. Borg, *Meeting Jesus Again for the First Time: The Historical Jesus and the Heart of Contemporary Faith* (Harper Collins, 1995).

Chapter 1

CONVERSION:
moving toward jesus

Walk in the light of Christ,
and learn to trust in his wisdom.

—from the Rite of Christian Initiation of Adults

Just as we only come to know our true selves
by letting our selves be known in and through Christ,
so, too, can we only come to know
the true events of our time
in and through the Christ-event.
Our true story reveals itself
through the story of Christ.
The story of Christ is therefore
not "the greatest story ever told,"
but the only story ever told.
It is the story from which all other stories
receive their meaning and significance.
The story of Christ makes history real.

—Henri J. M. Nouwen

The Christian knows that Christ has been working
in humanity for twenty centuries
and that the person that is converted to Christ
is the new human being that society needs
to organize a world according to God's heart.

—Oscar Romero

Look to Christ

Disc 1 • Track 1

Look to Christ to be your light; fol - low.

Leave be - hind your for - mer self and

live. Don't look back, don't

be a - fraid; fol - low.

Come to Christ, walk with Christ, and live.

Who is the one who sees everything we say and do?
Who is the one who knows us and still forgives?
Who is the source and fountain of grace that heals our thirst?
Jesus, the Christ: the Water of Life and Love.

Who is the one who gives new sight to all who are blind?
Who is the one who washes and makes us new?
Who is the one who opens our eyes that we may believe?
Jesus the Christ: the Living Light of God.

Who is the one who weeps for us? Who can this be?
Who is the one who takes the stone away?
Who is the one who cries to us all to come out and live?
Jesus the Christ: Resurrection and Life for all.

Text: David Haas
Tune: David Haas
© 2007, GIA Publications, Inc.

For Catholics and mainline Christian churches, the word "conversion" is one that does not get thrown around or used in conversation very often. We usually think of conversion when we think of one who is a "convert"; one who moves from one Christian tradition to another. For those of us who are called to follow Jesus, conversion is more than a change or direction of belief, but a fundamental *transformation*—a commitment and surrender that is total. We not only move from unbelief to belief, but we embrace the way of life that such a belief requires.

To offer our life to Jesus means we must not "look back" at old patterns, but rather face a new future unafraid. It demands leaving behind those things that are in conflict with new possibilities, growth and a transformed life in Jesus. In this context conversion means we "look to Christ" in everything we say and do; it means we "look to Christ" when discerning our choices; it means we "look to Christ" as the primary model for our lives as disciples. To "look to Christ" is a life response; a radical change of heart.

- Why is surrender to Christ so difficult?
- What gets in the way?
- What do we need to leave behind to follow Christ more faithfully?
- What are the signs and miracles in our lives that reveal Christ?

Christ Jesus,
come and push aside
the walls that keep you far away;
come and confront our fear
and help us to follow you
with all that we have,
with all that we are,
with all that we hope to become.
Come now,
and free our hearts to let go
and let you dwell in us
and take us over,
so we may be new again,
for the first time.

Amen.

We Are One in the Lord

Disc 1 • Track 2

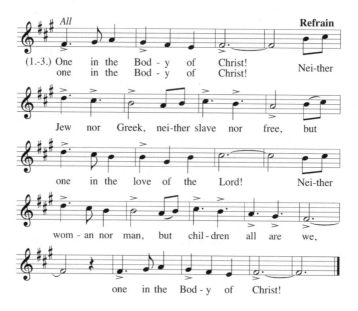

God alone has saved us: we are one in the Lord!
Calling us to be holy: we are one in the Lord!
Death now has been shattered; we are risen to new life:
one in the Body of Christ!

Called as your sons and daughters: we are one in the Lord!
Builders of the kingdom: we are one in the Lord!
Light to all the nations, bound together by our love:
one in the Body of Christ!

We are no longer strangers: we are one in the Lord!
Members of the body: we are one in the Lord!
Alien no longer, we are one with the saints:
one in the Body of Christ!

We will now follow Jesus: we are one in the Lord!
Chosen for salvation: we are one in the Lord!
If we die we shall live, if we endure we will reign
as one in the Body of Christ!

Text: Based on Galatians 3:28; 2 Timothy 1:9–10; 2:10–11; Ephesians 2:19; David Haas
Tune: David Haas
© 1981, GIA Publications, Inc.

To live as Christians in unity, to be one in the Lord, requires the ongoing work of conversion, which is not being born again, but rather, to be born again, again, and again. In other words, we who live under the shadow of the cross of Jesus are called each day to look at the world, our relationships, our families, and ourselves in a new way. We will be more one in Christ when we stop trying so hard to conform to a rigid and false sense of unity, and instead recognize our common need for Christ to reign over and guide our lives. The call to be holy is not the foolish goal to be perfect but to face honestly the real truth that without Christ we can accomplish nothing. This is where unity is found, in our common humanity and our desperate need for healing and wholeness; in our common failures and struggles; and in our humble recognition that the fullness of life can only be found in being attentive to the presence of Christ in the common journey in each other—the Body of Christ.

Unity: being one in the Body of Christ. It will be found only when we cease trying to force each other to change, get out of each other's way, and finally see that we are all children of God in our own unique and wonderful way, all bound together by the love of the Lord.

- How can we seek Christ more clearly in our desire to be holy?
- Where and with whom do we experience ourselves as one in the Lord?
- How can we celebrate the differences in our relationships and still find a common direction in our spiritual lives?

Christ Jesus,
we know that you call all of us,
with our sameness and differences,
to come together, find solidarity,
and celebrate being your hands,
feet, and heart to the world.
You have shown us the way;
you have given us a path that is clear.
Come and open our eyes
to see what you have in store for us.
Come and free our hearts
from the stiffness that keeps us
separated and isolated.
Bring us together, one in you.

Amen.

ALL I WANT

Disc 1 • Track 3

All I want, all I need is to know Christ; to fol-low the Lord. I press on t'ward the goal, the prize of the call of God.

Everything but this is loss and worthless to me;
after gaining Christ, there is nothing,
nothing that I need.

I want to know the Lord, and the power of God's love;
Becoming like Christ in death, I may rise,
rise to new life.

Forgetting what lies behind, forward I'll go.
I press on to make it my own;
Christ Jesus made me whole.

Text: Based on Philippians 3:8–14; David Haas
Tune: David Haas
© 2000, GIA Publications, Inc.

The text for this song is from Philippians, a beautiful reflection and celebration of belief, commitment, and grace found in Gospel living. The freedom and liberation found in these words are usually attractive to all of us as a pure path in our ongoing conversion and transformation as we try to follow Christ. However, to be able to continue on this path requires a posture of joy.

Such a joyful life response is not possible if we see it as a halfway proposition. This is an act of desire combined with discipline. We not only choose Christ; we choose to do so in a focused way, recognizing the need to not look back, but to press on and make this faith real and central in our lives.

We can only seek to be whole in Christ Jesus when we first recognize the fact that we are, indeed, not whole, but broken. We can only celebrate the prize of the call of God when we cast away all of the other callings in our lives that seduce us into making choices that are convoluted by our neediness, ego, and pride. All these things get in our way, but we can move through them when we have the discipline, combined with joy, to see Christ and the life that he has promised as our goal, our life, and our song.

- What are our desires?
- What are the blocks that keep us from fulfilling these desires?
- What does Jesus offer beyond our personal desires and wants?
- What brokenness keeps us from achieving our greatest desires?

Christ Jesus,
we long to know you,
to feel you close,
to cast away all things and choices
that keep us from reaching you.
We want to know you
and your power in our lives.
We want to be more like you,
and we desire to follow your path
of suffering and rising to a new way
of living.
Come now,
give us the strength to move forward,
to find the wholeness
that only you can give.

Amen.

Present among Us

Disc 1 • Track 4

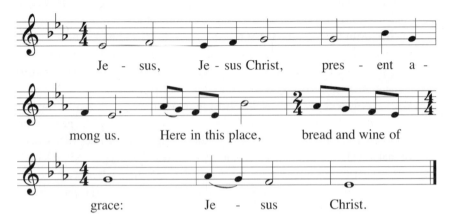

Je - sus, Je - sus Christ, pres - ent a -
mong us. Here in this place, bread and wine of
grace: Je - sus Christ.

In the taking, in the blessing,
in the breaking, in the sharing—
here before you at this table,
now we dine with you.

In our singing, in our healing,
in our giving, in our loving—
here before you at this table,
now we dine with you.

In our searching, in our aching,
in our longing, in our grieving—
here before you at this table,
now we dine with you.

Text: David Haas
Tune: David Haas
© 2003, GIA Publications, Inc.

At the heart of our conversion comes the challenge to recognize, name, and celebrate that Jesus Christ is real and *present*, here and now. In the sacred meal of the Eucharist we stake a claim for this presence in a most compelling way. When we dine together at the Lord's supper, we do more than just recognize this presence in the sharing of bread and wine at liturgy; we connect it to all the activity of our ordinary—but at the same time—holy lives. When we give or experience forgiveness, we draw on the strength that the meal of the Eucharist gives us; when we search, ache, and even grieve in the midst of fear and confusion, we feed upon the hope which the simple sharing of bread and wine provides. When we rejoice in the lavish love of Christ at the table of our hopes and dreams, we commune with this presence and the most precious grace that it provides: a relationship with the paschal mystery beyond dogma, a tangible embrace with Jesus Christ who touches our lives in a personal way. In this act and because of it we live, die, and rise with Jesus, and thus we do more than merely survive. We live the gift of life in the fullness of Christ's love.

- Where do we find Christ's presence beyond the liturgy?
- What commitment are we making when we share in the Eucharistic meal?
- Where can we build tables in our lives that will give life and reality to the presence of Jesus?

Christ Jesus,
we know you are here.
We know and believe
that in the midst of all things—
good and bad, joyful and fearful,
in peace and in stress,
in birth and in death—you are here.
Help us to always remember
and name you as present with us
in our daily life,
in the ordinary and extraordinary,
whether alone,
or in the midst of loving relationships,
and even in places of fear.
May we always feed on your love,
for you are always present, always here.

Amen.

Chapter 2
incarnation:
celebrating the birth of Jesus

Christ became what we are
in order that we might become what he is.

−Saint Athanasius

We must not seek the child Jesus
in the pretty figures of our Christmas cribs,
We must seek him among the undernourished children
who have gone to bed tonight with nothing to eat,
among the poor newsboys
who will sleep covered with newspapers in doorways.

−Oscar Romero

Praying is first and foremost listening to Jesus,
who dwells in the very depths of your heart.

−Henri J. M. Nouwen

Be Born in Us Today

Disc 1 ● Track 5

1. Through the win-ter and the cold,
   our faith can weak-en and grow old;
   so we ache to find a song of a
   God, one to whom we can be-long.
   In-stead of pow-er shown as might,
   a ti-ny ba-by is your light;
   we find a child who sings the way,
   come now, be born in us to-day.

2. Christ-mas comes and Christ-mas goes,
   yet pain and vio-lence sad-ly grow.
   We cry and hurt, when will it end? Is there a
   sav-ior, a mes-si-ah whom you'll send?
   We pray in hope, please hear our cry,
   or is the sto-ry just a lie?
   We need the child to show the way,
   come now, be born in us to-day.

3. In this time of joy and cheer,
   we find re-sent-ment, bound by fear;
   called to be-lieve, but we are blind, give us a
   rea-son, a life-line we can find.
   Poi-soned by self-ish-ness and hate,
   how much long-er must we wait?
   This child brings life to our de-cay,
   come now, be born in us to-day.

4. Give us a sign that you are real,
   numb though we are, help us to feel.
   There's on-ly one gift that we need, a man-ger,
   too, where all can come and feed.
   We need to know we're not a-lone,
   a place of safe-ty, a home.
   Al-though the cross is here to stay,
   come now, be born in us to-day.

Text: David Haas
Tune: David Haas
© 2001, GIA Publications, Inc.

Ironically, Christmas seems to be a mixed soup of celebration and joy alongside sadness, loneliness, and even despair. It should make us quake to know that this season of new birth, joy, and family ties is also fraught with extreme loneliness, isolation, and even suicide.

The season of Lent is not when we first confront the Paschal Mystery. Rather, it begins right away in the mystery of the incarnation, at the very birth of Jesus. Our faith encourages us to not lose heart. In the midst of the sadness that often contradicts this season we can discover the hope, taste the promise, and embrace the compassion that Jesus reveals to us in our common human story, consecrating it as holy, blessed, and part of the journey of salvation. This Jesus comes to us, not in a grand and majestic procession, but in the simplicity of a child with all the hope and possibility that each newborn brings. It is in this amazing simplicity that we can find Christmas again, and more importantly, discover Jesus born again in our hearts.

- How do we try to hide from darkness when our surroundings and situations expect only light?
- How attentive are we to the pain and sadness that often runs parallel to the joy of this season?
- What things get in our way and keep us from celebrating the fullness of Christ becoming incarnate in our lives?

Christ Jesus,
come and be born in us today.
Come and brighten up our darkness
with the simplicity of your newborn light.
Come, be messiah! Come, be savior!
Come, be here with us, today.
We know and believe that only you
can help us be born again.
So come now,
and restore in us a joy that will last,
a joy that is honest,
and a joy that will be the result
of our compassion and care for each other
and for ourselves.

Amen.

Child of Joy and Peace

Disc 1 • Track 6

1. Child of joy and peace, born to ev - 'ry
2. Born a - mong the poor on a sta - ble
3. Ev - 'ry child needs bread till the world is
4. Son of pov - er - ty, shame us till we

race— by your star, the wise will know you,
floor, cold and raw, you know our hun - ger,
fed; you give bread, your hands en - a - ble
see self - con - cerned, how we de - ny you,

East and West their hom - age show you, look in - to your
weep our tears and cry our an - ger— yet you tell us
all to gath - er round your ta - ble— Christ-mas must be
by our greed we cru - ci - fy you on a Christ-mas

face, child of joy and peace.
more, born a - mong the poor:
shared, ev - 'ry child needs bread.
tree, Son of pov - er - ty.

Text: Shirley Erena Murray; © 1992 Hope Publishing Company.
Tune: David Haas © 2000, GIA Publications, Inc.

It is awesome beyond comprehension that God would choose to become connected and intimate with us, and do so in a way that shatters all presumptions. Jesus, God's most-blessed Son, comes to us in beginnings that are painstakingly humble. God chooses to be part of us, to feel what we feel, to struggle with our struggles, and to intentionally show up in the most impoverished setting: a stable floor, among the poor in a cold, dark, and forgotten place, amidst grave poverty. This is not a place, one would think, in which God would choose to become present to us. But this is exactly where the child of joy and peace *should* be found: with us, in the poor places where we experience the profound loss of many things, some material, and for most of us, the loss of the spiritual in our lives.

To be among the poor, the hungry, the abused, and the impoverished is to truly see the most youthful and passionate face of God. Here we see a child unaware of how awful its surroundings, very much alive in every way. What will our response be? Will we embrace the surroundings as gift and possibility for new life and love? Or will we be blinded by all that we have, and more importantly, by all that we still want, thus crucifying all of the previous non-material gifts that we should be giving and receiving? When our Christmas trees begin to dry out and the branches become brittle and fall to the floor, we toss out the tree. What else might we be tossing out?

- How do we experience poverty? Is Christ there?
- How can we be more attentive to the presence of pain during this season?
- What are some practical ways in which we can be with those who are poor?
- How do we become the hands and heart of Christ?

Christ Jesus,
you are born again and again in our lives.
Help us to see your birth
in the faces of those in whom we least expect
to find you.
Help us be bread for the poor;
help us make your nativity the hope for all.
Help us never to forget you,
help us never to deny you;
help us always celebrate you here,
new, alive, and with us.

Amen.

The Encounter

Disc 1 ● Track 7

1. Where shep - herds late - ly knelt, and
2. In that un - like - ly place I
3. How should I not have known I -
4. Can I, will I for - get how

kept the an - gel's word, I come in half - be -
find him as they said: sweet new born Babe, how
sai - ah would be there, his pro - phe - cies ful -
Love was born and burned its way in - to my

lief, a pil - grim strange - ly
frail! And in a man - ger
filled? With pound - ing heart, I
heart— un - asked, un - forced, un -

stirred; but there is room and
bed: a still small Voice to
stare: a Child, a Son, the
earned, to die, to live, and

wel - come there for me.
cry one day for me.
Prince of Peace— for me.
not a - lone for me?

Text: Jaroslav J. Vajda; © 1986 by Concordia Publishing House.
Tune: David Haas; © 2001, GIA Publications, Inc.

Generally speaking, there seems to be an absence of awe in our lives. This is often the reason why many ask for more mystery in our liturgy and other common rituals, as there is a deep yearning for a sense of the transcendent. For some, there seems to be a continual search for the "extra" ordinary or the paranormal to ignite our spiritual juices, to help us feel a sense of the holy. In other words, we sometimes think that if we can somehow capture a profound experience that is outside the bounds of what seems normal, then we can feel connected to God.

When we become concerned with such things, we lose the opportunity to renew our sense of awe and wonder in the midst of the most simple, ordinary, human, and engaging encounters; for it is in these most common experiences that we see the divine working and stirring. God's way is constantly being communicated in the most simple and ordinary, and here we see it in the presence of a birth.

Like the storyteller in this song, we, too, have things happening all around us. If we are paying attention, we will be moved and taken up by what we see, hear, touch, and taste. Here we see how God pulls us into the entire mystery of Christ without our asking for it, and without our being able to explain it. Yet the reign of God comes to birth, and the dying and rising of Jesus is perfectly seen and foretold, all in the most simple and awesome event of a birth.

- What does the nativity story teach us about how we experience Jesus?
- What does this mystery of the incarnation say to our own life stories?
- What are some of the most unlikely places and relationships that bring Jesus to birth in our lives?

Christ Jesus,
you are here, with us,
in the most unlikely times and places,
yet we forget to pay attention.
Come now
and open our eyes and hearts once again
to see your awesome story unfold.
Come now and open our senses
so that we can once again feel our hearts pounding
in the gift of your presence.
Come now, be the Child of God,
So that we may become
children of God.

Amen.

CHAPTER 3
DISCIPLESHIP:
foLLOWING tHe way of jesus

The Christian must remember
that he is likely to be
the only copy of the gospels
that the non-Christian will ever see.

—*Phillip Scharper*

We must choose sides, not between nations,
but between the world's way and Christ's way.
The world hates; God loves.

—*Dorothy Day*

For disciples, saying "yes" to Jesus Christ
means that they abandon themselves to God
and give loving assent to all that he has revealed.

—*United States Conference of Catholic Bishops*

To Be a Servant

Disc 1 • Track 8

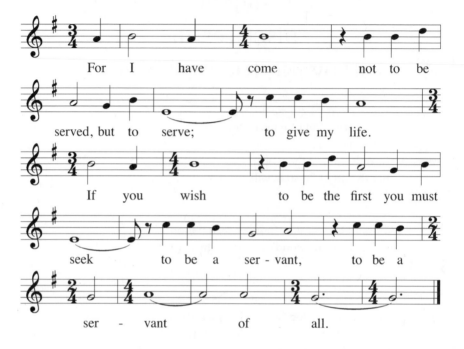

Can you drink the cup that I must drink;
are you willing?
Can you be baptized like I have been baptized?
Are you able? Are you able?

For to sit at my right hand or at my left,
is not for me to give.
But for those for whom it has been prepared,
it will be given. It will be given.

Text: Based on Mark 10:35–45; Matthew 15:21–27; Luke 14:25–33; David Haas
Tune: David Haas
© 2000, GIA Publications, Inc.

To serve in the spirit of Jesus means to give passionately and totally without reserve, qualification, or condition. Results often seem to occur when it is costly, often with consequences. With Jesus, it meant that everything was at risk, including his life. The same is true for us.

If we seek ministry or service as a means to an end, we have it wrong. To serve as Jesus did means being willing to experience and accept the journey, wherever it may take us. We are called to resist the common desire to rise above another, to acquire, win, achieve, grasp, and succeed. Jesus teaches us that we must abandon this course of action; we are actually called to descend and let another pass.

This is ministry with integrity. This is ministry that is in keeping with God's call. It is hard, but it is in the spirit of Jesus. It is what our baptism means and calls us to. We refuse to duck and hide when the baptismal water comes our way. Rather, we dive into the water and respond with the entirety of our lives. Are we able?

- What cup do we need to drink in order to serve?
- To what need and service is our baptism calling us?
- Who are the models and mentors of service in our lives?

Christ Jesus,
you call us to take a step back,
to slow down,
and to let you direct our service.
We need you to guide our path.
Lead us all to accept
and embrace the challenges
that you have placed before us.
We want to serve.
Show us the way,
a way that will build up another,
a way that will reveal you in all things,
a way that will place your people
front and center of all our concern, passion,
and care.

Amen.

We Have Been Told

Disc 1 ● Track 9

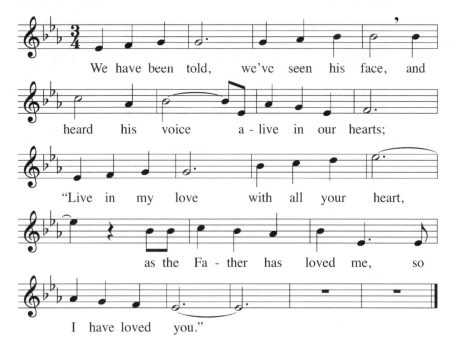

We have been told, we've seen his face, and heard his voice a - live in our hearts; "Live in my love with all your heart, as the Fa - ther has loved me, so I have loved you."

I am the vine, you are the branches.
And all who live in me will bear great fruit.

You are my friends, if you keep my commands.
No longer slaves: I call you friends.

No greater love is there than this:
to lay down one's life for a friend.

Text: Based on John 15:9–17; David Haas
Tune: David Haas
© 1983, GIA Publications, Inc.

The voice of God can be very difficult to hear, as there are many voices that crowd our minds and hearts. To be attentive to the voice of wisdom is at the heart of discernment. As people of faith, even when our spirit is diminished or beaten down, we have to hang on and cling to the promise, even if sometimes we do so by our fingernails. We must know and believe the promise that we are loved in a most profound and unconditional way. It really is true that there is no greater love than the one we find in God through Jesus. But we cannot receive this love without living and loving with all our heart because the love of Christ is boundless; it is for all. If we have listened well, heard his voice, and seen his face, we will see it in everyone, because each and every one of us is a child of God.

- When have we been blessed to experience this amazing love of Christ?
- To what degree are we willing to express our love?
- Where in our lives do we see ourselves being called to love so intensely right now?

Christ Jesus,
we have been told,
and we have heard your voice
of unconditional love over and over.
What an amazing gift you give to us,
to love us so totally.
Free us from the limitations
that keep us from loving your people
with the same sense of abandon.
Come now,
and instill in us the voice
and life
that will be a worthy expression of love
to all those in our lives,
unyielding,
unconditional.

Amen.

THAT YOU MIGHT HAVE LIFE

Disc 1 • Track 10

I have come to you that you might have life, life to the full, life for the world.

Come, enter through me; you will be safe in peace.
Walk in the light; darkness will be no more.
I will laugh and cry with you, and walk lonely roads with you.

Text: Based on John 10:10–12:46; David Haas
Tune: David Haas
© 1989, GIA Publications, Inc.

When the question arises as to why Jesus came to earth, the most common answer is that he came to die for our sins. It is interesting to note that Jesus never says, "I have come to die for your sins" in the Gospels. But here is an example of one of the powerful ways in which Jesus does answer the question: "I have come that you might have life." Yet, Jesus' answer does not end here, as he proclaims life to the full.

Such a notion of having life to the full seems more exquisite than we can imagine. Far too often, we live halfway; far less than a hundred precent, most of the time. Yet we want fulfillment, serenity, confidence, and wholeness. While these things may seem unattainable, they are not if we redefine what these things are and what they mean for us. They are defined differently from person to person, but the path is still the same.

To attain this level of peace and fullness is very simple: we just have to allow Christ to enter our hearts and be open to his grace and spirit to move and change our hearts. Most of all, it means being open to the belief that such a life is not some surreal fantasy. It is a gift, and most definitely real. There is no other way with Christ.

- What would life to the full feel like?
- Where and when do we find life to be a true adventure?
- How can we live our lives to the full for the sake of others?

Christ Jesus,
you are the source
of all that makes us whole,
of all that we can accomplish.
With you by our side,
there is nothing that we cannot do.
Be with us on our journey.
Be with us as we seek you
with every ounce of energy we have
to be your servants to the world
so that all may know
the completeness of joy
that comes from you alone.

Amen.

Song of the Temptation

Disc 1 • Track 11

1. From the riv - er to the des - ert, for - ty days that
2. "If you are the one God choos - es, you can turn these
3. "If you are the one God of - fers, leap in - to the
4. "If you are the one God prom - ised, you could still bow
5. Since we are the ones you gath - er, and from sin and

give no rest; fast and pray and wait and wres - tle,
stones to bread. See, the chil - dren yearn and hun - ger,
an - gels' hands. Show your pow - er and your glo - ry,
down to me. Look at all the wealth of na - tions,
death have freed, Je - sus, know - ing all our weak - ness,

face the Ad - ver - sar - y's test; Prince of Peace and
by your deeds the poor are fed." "—Don't you know that
then be - lief will sweep the land.""—Don't you know that
I will give you all you see." "—Don't you know that
now at God's high al - tar plead. For we know that

Prince of Dark - ness meet in lone - ly
it is writ - ten: No one lives by
it is writ - ten: Do not tempt the
it is writ - ten: Wor - ship God and
it is writ - ten that your grace is

wil - der - ness.
bread a - lone."
Lord your God."
God a - lone."
all we need.

Text: Based on Luke 4:1–13; Sylvia Dunstan
Tune: David Haas
© 1991, 2000, GIA Publications, Inc.

This is a story of the conversion and transformation that Jesus himself experiences. Yes, it is true. In the solitude of the desert he confronts all of the usual temptations, seductions, and more that come with power, leadership, responsibility, and yes, ministry. When we are told we are chosen in the sense of divine vocation it is easy to get a swelled head and become misled by power. When we see ourselves as a solution or a savior, we think that we can jump over buildings in a single bound. When we are offered what seems to be unlimited riches and influence, it is all too easy to be seduced into a delusion of our own importance and fall into the trap of invincibility.

Jesus is confronted here with all of these things and much more. His transformation requires him to do more than just denounce the temptations put before him. His sacred calling is to respond with wisdom and teaching: "No one lives by bread alone," "Do not tempt the Lord your God," and the ultimate insight that guides who we are and whose we are: "Worship God and God alone."

As wonderful as it is to be God's people, we are not God. It is by God's grace alone that we are able to live fully and rise again, again, and again. Loneliness, solitude, and walking in the desert need not be a journey of isolation, but rather a path of prayer and ongoing conversion, where we wrestle with a mysterious and loving God.

- Do we make time in our lives to be still, alone, and truly face our fears?
- What are the seductions and temptations that we need to renounce?
- Do we give ourselves enough time to reflect on our calling?

Christ Jesus,
as one who faced his own demons,
you know our struggles very well.
We need the strength
that comes from your strength
to say no to power.
We need the courage
that comes from your courage
to say no to self-interest.
We need the grace
that comes from you alone
to know that we need your presence
through every step and challenge that we face.
Come and be that strength for us.

Amen.

BLEST ARE THEY

Disc 1 • Track 12

Re - joice! and be glad!

Bless-ed are you, ho - ly are you, Re -

joice! and be glad!

Yours is the king-dom of God!

Blest are they, the poor in spirit,
theirs is the kingdom of God.
Blest are they, full of sorrow,
they shall be consoled.

Blest are they, the lowly ones,
they shall inherit the earth.
Blest are they who hunger and thirst,
they shall have their fill.

Blest are they who show mercy,
mercy shall be theirs.
Blest are they, the pure of heart,
they shall see God!

Blest are they who seek peace;
they are the children of God.
Blest are they who suffer in faith,
the glory of God is theirs.

Blest are you who suffer hate,
all because of me.
Rejoice and be glad, yours is the
kingdom;
shine for all to see.

Text: Based on Matthew 5:3–12; David Haas
Tune: David Haas
© 1985, GIA Publications, Inc.

There are several biblical scholars who claim that this section of the Sermon on the Mount was not a single speech that Jesus delivered but rather a power-packed summary of his entire ministry and vision of the Kingdom of God. This is more than a blueprint for living a righteous and upright life; it is an ongoing reflection and inventory of our entire life in Christ.

We are asked to see people as Jesus sees them, and to see ourselves as one with them in their journey. The poor, the sorrowful, the lowly, and the hungry; the merciful and pure of heart; the peacemakers and those who suffer—they are *all of us*.

Jesus does not offer a way around our struggles. Rather, he provides a way *through* and *with* the many terrors of life. To show who Jesus is, to make Jesus known, is to continually stay connected to the wisdom and challenge found in these proclamations and, without reserve, sing and celebrate the new life found here. We are both the givers and receivers of this good news, and Jesus is alive every time we stay true to the "curriculum" offered here. Blest are they, and blest are we.

- Is our personal vision in line with Jesus' vision?
- Are we living that way?
- How can we be more in solidarity with those who are at the center of Jesus' concern?
- In what ways are we being schooled to help build the Kingdom of God?

Christ Jesus,
you shower your blessing
upon all of us:
the poor and suffering,
the lonely and hungry,
those bound by guilt and shame,
those seeking justice and peace.
May our lives be a blessing
upon the world
through our choices and service
to those most in need:
the most vulnerable,
the most precious jewels
in God's fragile family.
Help us to rejoice and be glad
in the Kingdom you have prepared for us.

Amen.

Take Up Your Cross

Disc 1 • Track 13

If you lose your life for my sake, you will find it. If you want to save your life, let it go. Take up your cross, deny yourself: Come, follow me, follow me.

How will you profit by gaining the world,
while you forfeit all of your life?
What will you give in return?
What will you give in return?

Before I return in glory,
I will give you the gift of my love.
You will never taste death.
You will never taste death.

Text: Based on Matthew 16:24–28; David Haas
Tune: David Haas
© 2001, GIA Publications, Inc.

It is painfully difficult for us to believe that we should deliberately choose to lose our lives and, by doing so, find what it means to be alive. It just does not make sense. No wonder Jesus had so many enemies after saying illogical and crazy things like this. Once again, Jesus is offering us a path filled with paradox.

Self-denial and intentionally choosing to take up a cross do not seem to be in our self-interest, yet crosses always seem to find us. Life is a constant stream of crosses that come our way, and it certainly was the case for the people Jesus encountered before he took up the ultimate cross of his own sacrifice and death.

Suffering is a mystery, a puzzle, one that Jesus is constantly asking us to accept and live. To follow the path that Jesus walked requires courage not to shrink from it, and to somehow discover the healing and wholeness that comes from surrendering our own desires in order to be attentive to the pain and anguish of others.

To take up our own cross is to choose life in the midst of death, hope in the midst of hopelessness, light in the midst of darkness, and healing in the midst of pain. It is to accept suffering as part and parcel of discipleship. To surrender fully to the cross and to rise again with Jesus is to accept God's presence in the midst of it all.

- What parts of our lives do we need to lose?
- What parts do we need to choose?
- How does the cross of Jesus become our cross?
- In what concrete ways can we renew our commitment to follow Jesus?

Christ Jesus,
we believe
that you give us a cross
as a gift
to enable us
to share in the freedom
that you alone can give.
Help us to let go of all the things
that keep us far from you.
Help us to embrace your cross
so that it may become our cross,
our gift, our hope,
and our path to new life.

Amen.

Do Not Let Your Hearts Be Troubled

Disc 1 • Track 14

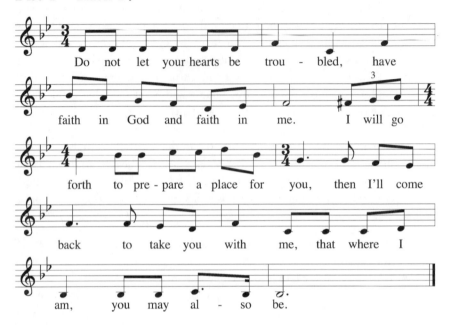

Do not let your hearts be trou - bled, have
faith in God and faith in me. I will go
forth to pre - pare a place for you, then I'll come
back to take you with me, that where I
am, you may al - so be.

In God's house there are many places
for you alone to dwell in safety.
You know the way to where I'll lead you,
if you are lost, I will show the way.

I am the way, the truth and the life,
only through me can you know what I know.
If you knew me, you would see the vision.
If you see me, you see your God.

The words I speak are not only of myself,
it is your God who lives within me.
If you believe that your God and I are one,
I will provide when you call my name.

Text: Based on John 14:1–3, 6–7, 10–14; David Haas
Tune: David Haas
© 1995, GIA Publications, Inc.

Jesus is with us. While he does not always fix things according to our blueprints, and while he does not seem to always prevent us from coming into harm's way, he is with us. Always. We need to cling fast to this most blessed assurance; we are invited to hang on to this by faith.

We are called to be attentive to that most profound presence of Christ, found not only in the tabernacle that holds the consecrated bread but also in the struggles and aches and pains of everyday life. Jesus is with us, preparing a place for us, and not just down the road, but right here, right now. We are given an ongoing place of safety, care, and deep abiding love.

Jesus says, "Where I am, you may also be." What an amazing act of generosity and faithfulness to us! To receive such an amazing gift compels us to return in kind, to give generously and faithfully to each other in lavish ways. To calm a troubled heart should be at the center of our stance toward each other, since it is, most profoundly, the stance of Jesus toward us.

- How can we free our troubled hearts to accept the care that Jesus gives?
- Where and when do we tend to be inattentive to the presence of Jesus?
- What are the places of safety that we are called to offer to another?

Christ Jesus,
we hold on to a world
of proof and facts
while you proclaim a world
of truth and life.
Help us to turn our hearts
over to your heart which sustains us,
to your life that is caught up
in reaching out and healing
the most troubled of hearts.
Help us to celebrate our faith,
which is you, and you alone.

Amen.

Song of the Lord's Command

Disc 1 • Track 15

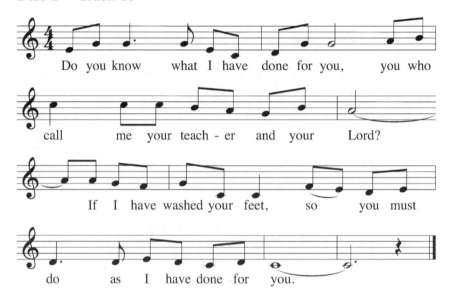

Do you know what I have done for you, you who
call me your teach-er and your Lord?
If I have washed your feet, so you must
do as I have done for you.

What I am doing now you do not know,
but after a time has gone by,
you will understand.

Don't you understand what I must do?
If you would be mine,
then I must bend to wash your feet.

I have given to you an example;
what I have done for you,
you must do for one another.

Text: Based on John 13:1–5, 15:12–14, 16; David Haas
Tune: David Haas
© 1997, GIA Publications, Inc.

John's Gospel does not contain the traditional rendering of the Last Supper that we see in Matthew, Mark, and Luke. Rather, John has the story of the washing of feet, which many have come to name as "John's Eucharist."

This ritual, which many faith communities celebrate on Holy Thursday, is a powerful action of Jesus' philosophy of service: it is to inconvenience oneself for the sake of others and to bend low and lift up servants to become those to be served. It is to be disciples for all God's children, without distinction, honoring their stories and dreams and to be a source of healing and hope for all of us desperate for good news.

Washing feet is the activity and priority for all who would be servants—ministers of healing and promise. Jesus may sit high, but he always looks low. Any exaltation of Jesus is predicated by his commitment to being a servant, washing feet, and healing wounds—all directed to the praise of the Creator God. We are called to do the same.

- How do we imitate the way of Jesus in our stance of ministry and service?
- What does the example of Jesus compel us to do?
- Where do we find examples of Jesus' invitation to service?

Christ Jesus,
you have given us an example
beyond compare;
you have shared with us
your embrace of all people.
All are holy,
all our blessed in your sight.
Come and help us
to bend our feeble knees
to be one, eye-to-eye
with those in need of your love,
your care,
and your compassion.
You are our teacher and Lord,
and we know
what you have done for us.
Help us to do the same
for each other.

Amen.

Chapter 4

journey:
walking by faith with jesus

It seems that we Christians
have been worshipping Jesus' journey
instead of doing his journey.

–Richard Rohr, OFM

If, then, you are looking for the way by which you should go,
take Christ, because he himself is the way.

–Saint Thomas Aquinas

To know Christ is to know God.
Christ is the homily
that keeps explaining to us continually
that God is love,
that God is power,
that the Spirit of the Lord is upon Jesus Christ,
that he is the divine Word,
God's presence among us.

–Oscar Romero

I WILL GIVE YOU REST

Disc 1 • Track 16

1. Take my yoke up - on you,
2. Come a - way, dis - ci - ple;
3. Trust - ing and re - turn - ing,
4. When your world is chang - ing
5. When the night grows long - er,

all who la - bor long. I am al - ways with you,
come, re - treat a while. I will trav - el with you,
you shall grow in strength. I am al - ways with you,
at a breath - less pace, I am al - ways pres - ent,
and the end is near, I am your com - pan - ion,

I am al - ways with you. Learn my way of liv - ing,
I will trav - el with you, bless-ing des - ert plac - es,
I am al - ways with you; since my love de-signed you,
I am al - ways pres - ent, cen - ter in life's turn-ing,
I am your com - pan - ion, hope in joy or sor - row,

sim - ple and for - giv - ing,
fill - ing Sab - bath spac - es,
seek and I will find you, 1.–5. and
light in la - bor's learn - ing,
home be - yond to - mor - row,

I will give you rest, and I will give you rest.

Text: Based on Matthew 11:28–30; Ruth Duck; © 1996 The Pilgrim Press.
Tune: David Haas; © 2005, GIA Publications, Inc.

Our lives really do seem at times to move at a breathless pace. When we move and live with a sense of frantic frenzy, important things are, at best, put aside, and often forgotten altogether. Sometimes we deliberately choose to over-schedule, overdo, overextend, overachieve—that way we do not have to face certain things that continually challenge us, hoping that they will go away.

Christians are asked to slow down and stop once in a while to reflect and pray. Those of us who follow Jesus are reminded that no matter the distractions, no matter the crazy pace of our lives or the degree of our anxiety, no matter how frightening the loneliness can feel, we are never alone. "I am always with you." "I will travel with you." "I am always present." "I am your companion." These are more than nice phrases to comfort us. These are words and promises that we can count on. The result is a holy rest that renews us.

- Why are we so afraid to slow down? What would we find if we did?
- Who seems to always be present and faithful in our lives?
- How can we step away from the race and, as the song says, "retreat a while" with Jesus?

Christ Jesus,
you are always here,
always making the journey with us,
always present,
always walking the lonely roads
that we walk.
Do not stop your relentless
pursuit of us;
do not suspend your precious companionship.
We need you to always believe in us,
even when we forget to stop,
take a breath, and drink you in.
Keep us busy,
for we have your work to do.
But at the same time,
keep reminding us
that we need to stop once in a while
and sit with you.

Amen.

You Alone Are the Word

Disc 1 • Track 17

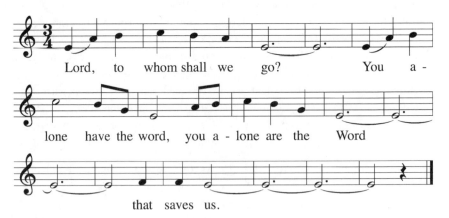

Lord, to whom shall we go? You a-
lone have the word, you a-lone are the Word
that saves us.

Deep in our longing, you know our searching,
then why do you hide your face?
Come be our answer, God give us an answer
to all of our crying and tears!

Here in our desert, terror surrounds us,
in anguish we call on your name!
Hear us and listen; O God, do you listen
to questions we cannot bear?

Fearful, uncertain, feeble and trembling,
we reach for your hand to heal!
Come be Messiah, are you Messiah
to all our broken dreams?

Text: Based on John 6; David Haas
Tune: David Haas
© 1988, GIA Publications, Inc.

Do we sometimes ask too much of Jesus? We are always looking for answers, and our life of prayer seems especially active when our lives are in crisis. We tend to reach out, or rather *cry* out, when we hit a wall of hopelessness and anxiety. It could be seen as an irony to honestly admit that it is when Jesus seems most *absent* that we ache for his presence most intensely.

When all seems lost, when everything seems to point in a direction of despair, we lament. And we should. We should not be afraid to lament, for it is at the heart of what it means to be human, alive, and breathing. The prayer of lament is the most honest prayer that we offer, and the Gospels tell us that Jesus did the same at the most difficult moments of his life and ministry—most certainly when all seemed lost at the cross.

Senseless violence, abuse, neglect, poverty, isolation, discrimination, loss, death, war, destruction—all these evils and more cry out for reasonable people to be angry and frustrated; determined to shake our fists at God and the so-called "good news" that is promised to us. These inclinations should not be denied, but rather embraced and voiced.

While most of us were taught to believe that we should never express anger at God, we need to remember that God is strong enough, wise enough, and yes, loving enough to handle and manage our anger. The love of God shown to us in Jesus Christ understands and laments with us. Jesus may not give daily concrete answers and solutions, but Jesus does offer a way through the darkness by giving us a word, rather the *Word*, the presence of God who understands our pain and fear. He never, ever leaves us alone, even when every sign seems to indicate otherwise.

- What things in our lives and the world lead us to lament?
- Why might we be hesitant to express our anger in prayer?
- What does our faith in Jesus offer during the greatest times of crisis?
- What do our crises teach us about how we can be connected to the crises of others?

Christ Jesus,
we look to you when all seems lost.
Deep down, we know
that you are always with us,
especially when all seems lost,
when life seems too unbearable.
Help us to express our fears,
our anger—to be in touch with

our feelings and emotions,
for they are a gift from you.
Help us to learn to lament in faith,
so that we may find comfort
and solace unsurpassed.

Amen.

Increase Our Faith

Disc 1 • Track 18

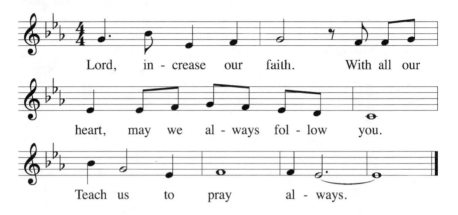

Lord, in - crease our faith. With all our
heart, may we al - ways fol - low you.
Teach us to pray al - ways.

So I say to you: "Ask, you will receive;
seek and you will find.
Knock, it shall be opened to you."

Whoever asks, they shall receive;
whoever seeks shall find.
Whoever knocks, the door will be opened.

If you, with all your sins, know how to give,
how much more will God
give to all those who cry from their hearts!

Text: Based on Luke 11:1–13, 17:5; David Haas
Tune: David Haas
© 1997, GIA Publications, Inc.

There is a saying somewhere that goes like this: "Faith is stepping out to the edge of the cliff of all that challenges us, and then taking one more step." What we *believe* is different than the things in which we trust and put our *faith*.

To have faith is to hold on to things that often seem irrational, impractical, and at times, filled with naiveté. Yet this is the path that Jesus is asking us to take; to really embrace this kind of faith. Here we as disciples ask Jesus to *increase* this faith, realizing that our prayer life, our ongoing conversation with God, is the way to do this.

We pray, sometimes often, but we still need a refresher course from time to time. Jesus teaches us to understand that our prayer needs to be centered in a faith that believes God is really on our side, that we are loved so much, and that God could not possibly abandon us. But how can this be so when we often pray for things that never seem to come true?

We can easily think that God, in many cases, really does not answer our prayer, but that is false. As people of faith, the practice of listening is so important. Prayer is not so much asking for things that we want, but rather, listening, in faith, to what God is trying to say to us. Jesus is a light for us in this regard: God *always* answers our prayers, but we forget to listen, and sometimes we do not like the answers. That is why we need to listen well to God's wisdom, not our own. This is what real prayer accomplishes. When we listen attentively, faith increases.

- In what ways do we rely on the kind of faith that listens to guide our lives and choices?
- Do we take the time to listen and discern when we pray?
- Where in the Gospels do we see Jesus listening attentively to the voice of God?

Christ Jesus,
we want to follow you
with all the faith we have,
with our hearts dedicated
to you and your cause.
Come now,
and strengthen our faith.
Come now,
and let your voice be heard
deep within,
and help us to listen, always.

Amen.

O Jerusalem

Disc 1 • Track 19

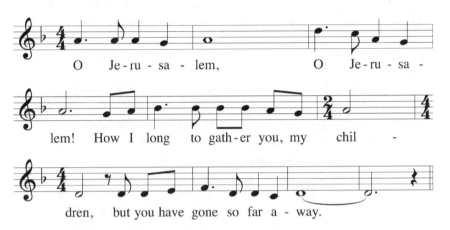

O Je-ru-sa-lem, O Je-ru-sa-lem! How I long to gath-er you, my chil - dren, but you have gone so far a - way.

Jerusalem, Jerusalem,
you scorn the ones that I have sent you.
Just as a mother cares for those beneath her wings,
I care for you, but you refuse!

Jerusalem, Jerusalem,
do not, do not weep for me.
Weep for yourselves and for the children not yet born,
for they will never come to birth!

Jerusalem, Jerusalem,
open your eyes, look now and see.
The reign you seek to find is here before your eyes;
it is within you, in your heart!

Text: Based on Luke 12:34–35, 17:20–21, 23:34–35; David Haas
Tune: David Haas
© 1997, GIA Publications, Inc.

Like us, Jesus laments. He laments for us time and time again in response to our struggles and failures. He laments for us when we refuse the gift of his love and protection, and when we deny and isolate ourselves from his care. He laments for us when we act blindly to the Reign of God that is emerging and flowering all around us, and when we anguish over his historical death on the cross (which consumes our piety) while remaining sightless and voiceless over the senseless cycle of death of our sisters and brothers right before our eyes day after day.

Jesus laments for us, knowing that we are too numb to realize that the possibilities for life, light, goodness, justice, and peace are all within our means to bring forth. He laments for us because his love for us is total, and because we forget to take our baptism seriously.

We are adopted daughters and sons of God, claimed for Christ and for his cause. When we say no to our baptismal call, Jesus laments. He is calling us not to a swim in a sea of guilt and shame, but rather toward an examination of conscience.

- What might Jesus lament in our time and place?
- Why do we sometimes close our eyes and ears to the call of Jesus?
- What concrete steps can we take to enliven our baptism?

Christ Jesus,
we know that your plans for us
come from a loving heart.
We also know
that we are far too often
blind to and careless with
the promises you give.
Come now,
open our eyes,
open our ears,
and open our hearts
to give you reason not to lament for us,
but rather,
to rejoice in us.

Amen.

In the Power of Christ

Disc 1 • Track 20

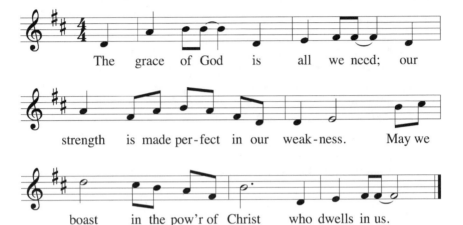

The grace of God is all we need; our strength is made per-fect in our weak-ness. May we boast in the pow'r of Christ who dwells in us.

I am content with weakness,
and insult, and hardship,
and distress, for the sake of Christ.
When I am weak then I am strong.
When I am weak then I am strong.

There is no other boast
than in the cross of Jesus,
through whom the world
has been crucified, for the glory of God.
When I am weak then I am strong.
When I am weak then I am strong.

Peace and mercy be to all who follow,
who follow to Israel of God.
May the grace of God be with you.
When we are weak then we are strong.
When we are weak then we are strong.

Text: Based on 2 Corinthians 12:9–10, Galatians 6:14–18; David Haas
Tune: David Haas
© 2003, GIA Publications, Inc.

The message here rides against all logic of how the world seems to operate, relationships are negotiated, and leadership is formed and disbursed. Jesus is constantly going against our usual assumptions and modes of operation: "the last shall be first," "unless a grain falls to the earth and dies," "love your enemies," "if someone strikes you on one cheek, offer them the other," "those who live by the sword die by the sword," and on, and on, and on.

Here Paul proclaims that "our strength is made perfect in our weakness," and "when I am weak then I am strong." This is radical stuff. But the grace of God can do strange and marvelous things. Jesus breaks through when we step back and embrace our weakness and fragile nature, when we are able to receive pain without returning evil for evil.

When we boast in the cross of Jesus, an instrument of death transformed into a path for healing and peace, we can rise above the pettiness and arrogance of competition, revenge, power, and selfishness. We can choose another way. We can choose the simple yet powerful path of love, mercy, and compassion. This is one of the blessings given to us by the cross of Jesus, "through whom the world has been crucified, for the glory of God," to break through the madness of the world and usher in the Reign of God.

- What is the grace of God and how does it operate in our lives?
- How can we as believers begin to renounce the demons of power and dominance and embrace Jesus' way?
- How can weakness strengthen our faith?

Christ Jesus,
you have given us
the example that we need.
You have shown us
that the way of weakness
is very strong, indeed.
Come strip away our false sense
of confidence, strength,
and power,
and infuse in us
the gentle acceptance of surrender.
Then we will be one with you.

Amen.

Christ Will Be Your Light

Disc 1 • Track 21

A - rise! A - rise! A - wake, rise up from the dead! Christ will shine! Christ will be your light!

Once you were lost in the darkness,
now you are in light in the Lord!
Live out each day as God's children,
live now as children of light!

Light shines forth every beauty,
justice and truth are revealed!
Seek the ways of the Lord!
Seek the way of light!

I am the light of the world!
I will make all things new!
Follow and you will find life,
follow and live in the light!

Text: Based on Ephesians 5:8–14, John 9:5b; David Haas
Tune: David Haas
© 1988, GIA Publications, Inc.

L iving in the light is hard. Staying asleep and living the path of least resistance is certainly uncontroversial, free of responsibility or challenge, and much more peaceful in the short run. But there is a relentless voice continually pushing and prodding us to rise up from the dead and live as children of light.

Some people prefer the dark. They often walk into a room and turn off every light. The opposite is also the case: some cannot bear even the tiniest bit of shade or darkness and always seek to escape the shadows.

As Christians, living in the light does not mean existing in a constant (and sometimes annoying) path of overbearing joy and naïve brightness. It should, however, call forth recognition that we belong to Christ, that this Christ walks with us as our companion, and that there is more good news than bad news.

Why? Because here, "the bible tells me so." Listen to these words: "Light shines forth every beauty, justice and truth are revealed." Maybe this is not always so, but hopefully each of us can recall when and where this has been true. Even in the face of realities that seem to proclaim the opposite—*especially* when this is the case—we are challenged to not let the demons and principalities of this world win. Even when it is hard, when all seems dark, we can walk passionately in the light.

Who is that light that shines brightly and walks with us? Christ Jesus. Where can we find this Jesus? In the midst of the many bright lights that surround us— each other.

- In the midst of hard times, where is the light constant in our life?
- Why do we sometimes stay asleep? How can we arise and stay awake in our faith?
- How are we working to reveal the justice and truth that Jesus brings?

Christ Jesus,
you are the light, the song that we sing,
and the justice and truth that we cling to.
Help us to seek you,
to follow, to live in your light:
a light that we know and believe
blazes through our unbelief.
Help us to let you
shine and break through
the darkness of our lives.

Amen.

Chapter 5

restoration:
from suffering to healing in Jesus

The world's pain is Christ's pain.
He knows every tear that falls.
We simply cannot live in this world
indifferent to its pain.
Rather, like Christ,
we must make the world's pain our pain.
We must experience a solidarity
with those Jesus described
as "the least of these."
We must see ourselves
in the tortured faces of those who experience loss.

–Daniel Vestal

God is to be found in all things,
even and most especially in the painful,
tragic, and sinful things,
exactly where we do not want to look for God.
The crucifixion…is at the same moment
the worst thing in human history
and the best thing in human history.

–Richard Rohr, OFM

If many have distanced themselves from the church,
it is precisely because the church has somewhat
estranged itself from humanity.
But a church that can feel as its own
all that is human
and wants to incarnate the pain, the hope,
the affliction of all who suffer and feel joy,
such a church will be Christ loved and awaited,
Christ present.
And that depends on us.

–Oscar Romero

The Water I Give

Disc 2 ● Track 1

All who drink the wa-ter I give will
nev-er thirst, the wa-ter I give will be a
foun-tain with-in you, giv-ing life.

Give us living water, we ask you, O Lord,
so that we may never thirst again.

All who drink the water of the earth will always thirst.
Drink of me and never thirst again.

The water I give will be a living spring,
leaping up to give eternal life.

Text: Based on John 4:13–15; David Haas
Tune: David Haas
© 1988, GIA Publications, Inc.

This song is from the story of the Samaritan woman who goes to the well to draw water. She ends up receiving something completely unexpected. Jesus exposes every single demon and flaw in her life, and she goes against type—she feels anything but shame. She experiences liberation and freedom. She announces to everyone the amazing and paradoxical experience of being found out, and praises God!

Far too often we drown in the waters of guilt, embarrassment, secrecy, and shame. Deep down, we all long for a fountain that will wash away our shame and send us on a current of healing and hope. In spite of any attempt on our part to hide, Jesus finds us. He sees us completely and remains totally in love with us. If that were not more than enough, this amazing love increases beyond anything imaginable.

This is exactly what makes Jesus different. He does not operate according to our rules or patterns. His love is deeper and flowers beyond any love we can ever hope to experience. The love of Christ is a fountain that never goes dry: it is eternal, without conditions, always faithful. No strings attached.

We are being called to join Jesus at the well and receive a shower of grace that will never go dry. We are invited to drink of this water and share its abundance with each other.

- What personal or national shame do we hold that cries out for cleansing?
- How can we be part of the fountain of life that Jesus offers to others?
- Where do we find fountains of life that nurture us spiritually?

Christ Jesus,
we thirst for so many things:
love, community,
security, self-worth,
wholeness, peace,
dignity, friendship,
and so much more.
In you we can find these things.
In you we can be made clean
by the fountain
of your love and compassion.
Come and lead us
to your well of grace and mercy,
so that we may never thirst again.

Amen.

He Healed the Darkness of My Mind

Disc 2 • Track 2

1. He healed the dark - ness of my mind the
2. Let oth - ers call my faith a lie, or
3. Ask me not how! But I know who has

day he gave my sight to me: It was not sin that
try to stir up doubt in me: Look at me now! None
o - pened up new worlds to me: This Je - sus does what

made me blind; It was no sin - ner made me see.
can de - ny I once was blind, and now I see.
none can do I once was blind, and now I see.

Text: Based on John 9:1–41; Fred Pratt Green; © 1982 Hope Publishing Company.
Tune: David Haas; © 1988, GIA Publications, Inc.

There is a subtle but important difference between being *cured* and *healed*. To be cured of something means it will never come back, never haunt one's life again. We usually see the story of Jesus and the man born blind as one of physical blindness and its cure. Jesus may or may not have literally *cured* the blind man of his physical blindness. We can argue back and forth about that, but to do so is to miss the point. What is important is that Jesus heals the blind man—and all of us—from living our lives in the dark. Jesus opens up new worlds for all of us who want to be free from the prison of darkness.

We sometimes do not really see the gift of life that God lays before us. Jesus opens up new worlds for all of us who feel trapped by sin, addictions, hate, anger, hopelessness, self-loathing, past choices, illness, loneliness, and fear of life.

This profound story of restoration is not about just one individual's *physical sight*, but more importantly, a birth of *insight*. Many people are never *cured* of their afflictions. But Jesus offers the promise of *healing* so that our afflictions will not consume us and win the day. It is a gift offered to all through the grace of faith.

- Where is darkness in our minds and hearts?
- How can we be more open to receive the healing that Jesus promises?
- How have we grown in seeing more clearly on our journey of faith?

Christ Jesus,
come and open our eyes,
our minds,
and our hearts
to receive the healing
that we so desperately need.
We believe beyond believing
that you are new sight
and new life for us
when we trust in you
and relinquish our lives
to your care and protection.
Come now,
heal the darkness of our lives.

Amen.

I Am the Resurrection

Disc 2 • Track 3

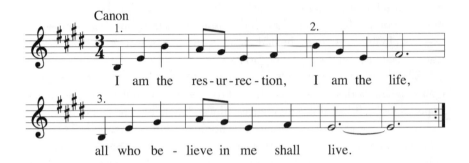

Text: Based on John 11:25–26; David Haas
Tune: David Haas
© 1988, GIA Publications, Inc.

This song comes from the amazing story of the raising of Lazarus. Prior to the hopeful words, "I am the resurrection, I am the life; all who believe in me shall live," we see a Jesus who weeps over the loss of his friend. True resurrection is preceded by sadness and death, even for Jesus.

While not a literal translation, the name Lazarus has been paraphrased to mean "God to the rescue!" Resurrection is far more than a bodily resuscitation. Resurrection is *rescue* from the many deaths that occur in our lives and all that would take us hostage. To embrace Jesus and his resurrection is to embrace hope. To embrace Jesus and his resurrection is to say loudly and clearly to the forces of sin and hate, "You will not prevail!"

The Lord's voice had to be loud and piercing in order for Lazarus to hear it through the rock and many bandages as well as the stench of death. The voice of Jesus promising resurrection is always trying to break through our own many barriers and tombs. At times, this voice is screaming "Come out!" to all of us bound by the bandages that have been imposed upon us, sometimes by our very selves.

Why is this refrain as heard on the recording sung over and over again, almost relentlessly? Because we usually do not hear it or get it at first; sometimes we need to be hit over the head, so to speak. We need to keep telling ourselves over and over again, however unbelievable, that this Jesus is our resurrection from every kind of death that surrounds us. Let's keep the song going in our heads and hearts, and hopefully, like Lazarus, we will be rescued and emerge rejoicing from our tombs.

- What are the things that keep us entombed?
- How can we remove our many bandages and step into the light of day?
- What is Jesus trying to say to us as we move from bondage to resurrection?

Christ Jesus,
there are so many things
that break us down,
where hope seems lost,
and survival seems
at its end.
Come now,
and rise in us today.

Come now,
and help us to be a part
of your resurrection song.
Come now,
and rescue us
once and for all.

Amen.

Jesus, Heal Us

Disc 2 • Track 4

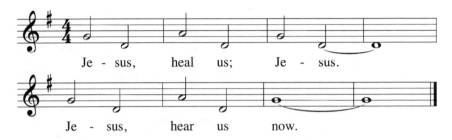

All who fear the Lord: wait for God's mercy.
All who love the Lord: Come, he will fill you.

All who know the Lord: follow his ways.
All who love the Lord: hope in his goodness.

All who trust the Lord, he will uphold you.
Let us cling to him, let us fall in the arms of the Lord.

Text: David Haas
Tune: David Haas
© 1988, GIA Publications, Inc.

The ache for healing lies within each and every one of us. Often we are not even aware that we are in need of healing. All of us hold wounds and scars deep within that are hard to even name or call to the surface. These bruises are not necessarily on our bodies, but upon our spirit, soul, and sense of joy.

Parents try to protect their children from being hurt, but it is often an exercise in futility or merely a delay. Hurt, pain, sadness, and cruelty will come to all of us no matter how we try to run from them, no matter how hard others try to isolate us from them. *Healing* is what we need, and it is a gift that Jesus gives us.

Part of the healing process entails our recognition that we are in a state of pain, and often that is the most difficult step. Jesus calls us to let go of our need to be strong, of choices that make us hardened and bitter, and our need to seek revenge. Healing says no to revenge and hate. Healing says we can stand up and feel again, knowing full well that suffering may again be lurking around the corner.

Throughout the Gospel stories Jesus offers this healing to Zaccheus, Mary Magdalene, and Peter; the woman with the hemorrhage, the woman at the well, the man born blind, and Lazarus—the list goes on. Jesus offers this healing to us as well.

- What parts of our life cry out for healing?
- Why do we sometimes choose revenge as a response to being hurt?
- Why do we sometimes seem afraid to receive the healing that Jesus can give?

Christ Jesus,
we need you to come and heal us.
Our lives often seem broken,
lost, and disoriented.
Come and restore us
and bring us back to life.
Come and heal our wounds
so we may have the health
and strength necessary
to face the trials and sufferings
that will most certainly
come our way.
Come, heal us. Now.

Amen.

Song of the Storm

Disc 2 • Track 5

1. The storm is strong; we face the wind. The water rises; waves crash in. Where are we now? Where will we be? There is no mercy on this sea.

2. But you, Christ, you are with us here. We turn to you in all our fear. The single word you say is "peace," and wind and waves and storm all cease.

3. Who can you be? What pow'r your say that even winds and sea obey? Remove our fear of death and harm. Give us your faith and still our storm.

Text: Based on Mark 4:35–41; Sylvia Dunstan
Tune: David Haas
© 1991, 2003, GIA Publications, Inc.

Water, as with all of the symbols of our faith, also has a dark side. Another song presented here (*The Water I Give*) portrays water as a symbol and force of love, acceptance, cleansing, and purification. This particular hymn acknowledges—as those who have experienced devastating floods or hurricanes know all too well—that water can be the enemy: a symbol of and force for destruction, fear, anxiety, and terror. But we need to move beyond the literal presentation of this Gospel story, for there is tremendous truth here. As Megan McKenna likes to say, "All stories are true, and some of them actually happened."

The important truth to this story is not necessarily what happened in the boat with Jesus and his disciples, but rather that storms rise up in all of our hearts at times. Sometimes the fear is so fierce we feel we are drowning. We feel alone, long for a small portion of peace, and ache for a power greater than ourselves to come in and intervene, to still the waters and make the waves quiet.

When we stop trying to steer the direction of our lives and allow the spirit of Christ to penetrate our hearts, we may find a clearing. But it requires faith. The waters of fear and death are always rising up somewhere. Who will we call upon to steer the boat?

- How do we cope when the water rises too high in our lives?
- What storms can we help calm in others?
- What parts of our lives do we need to hand over to the care of Jesus?

Christ Jesus,
we cry out to you,
"Where are you?"
We are drowning
and barely holding on.
We need you to keep us
from sinking into our despair.
Stay true to your word.
Help us to sing the faith
that we have seen
time and time again.
Come again,
and throw us a lifeline
filled with your love.

Amen.

Steal Away

Disc 2 ● Track 6

Steal a-way, steal a-way, steal a-way to Je-sus!

Steal a-way, steal a-way home, I ain't got long to stay here.

My Lord, he calls me,
he calls me by the thunder.
The trumpet sounds within my soul;
I ain't got long to stay here.

Green trees are bending,
poor sinners stand a-trembling.
The trumpet sounds within my soul;
I ain't got long to stay here.

My Lord, he calls me,
he calls me by the lightning.
The trumpet sounds within my soul;
I ain't got long to stay here.

Text: Traditional African-American spiritual
Tune: Traditional African-American spiritual; arr. David Haas
Arr. © 1997, GIA Publications, Inc.

The spirituals sung by African-American slaves in the nineteenth and twentieth centuries were more than just songs to strengthen them in the midst of their plight. Many of these spirituals were a sort of code used for communication while slave masters were close by. These songs were a way slaves strategized and encouraged each other in their dream of freedom. They sang these songs to Jesus, but also to each other.

To "steal away" was a metaphor about how they would make their way north to escape slavery. The phrase "I ain't got long to stay here" could be heard almost literally—that the singer is confident that slavery will not last much longer because hope and possibility are close by. To "steal away" is exactly that: to move from oppression to freedom, and Jesus was the path and guide in the slave's hope to be transformed into a new life.

The sound of the trumpet is the sound of resurrection, of healing, of the promise that life can have meaning and fulfillment. All of us need to listen to this song of the trumpet. It is here, sounding loudly to encourage us to move beyond our pain and suffering and rise above our sadness and mourning.

Resurrection is more than something that happened to the historical Jesus a long time ago. It is for all of us, right now. We "ain't got long to stay" in our bondage and shame. We can be set free. We can "steal away" to find and be with Jesus.

- In what ways do we feel enslaved?
- For what kind of freedom are we looking?
- What does the resurrection promise for our daily lives?

Christ Jesus,
you do not enslave us.
Often, we enslave ourselves,
but you provide a light and a way
to move beyond,
to move forward,
to embrace the freedom
that you have promised.
Come now,
set us free from our chains
and sound your trumpet
of hope and new life
in every part of our being.

Amen.

You Are Mine

Disc 2 • Track 7

I will come to you in the silence,
I will lift you from all your fear.
You will hear my voice, I claim you as my choice,
be still and know I am near.

I am hope for all who are hopeless,
I am eyes for all who long to see.
In the shadows of the night, I will be your light,
come and rest in me.

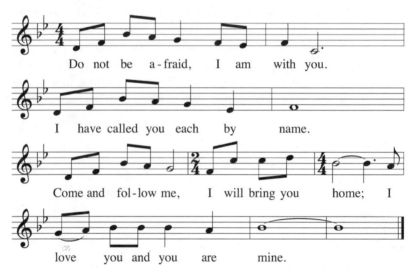

Do not be a-fraid, I am with you.
I have called you each by name.
Come and fol-low me, I will bring you home; I
love you and you are mine.

I am strength for all the despairing,
healing for the ones who dwell in shame.
All the blind will see, the lame will all run free,
and all will know my name.

I am the Word that leads all to freedom,
I am the peace the world cannot give.
I will call your name, embracing all your pain;
stand up, now walk, and live!

Text: David Haas
Tune: David Haas
© 1991, GIA Publications, Inc.

When all seems lost and the darkest voices haunt us, when we feel as though our sadness and grief are just too much, we stretch out our hands and cry from our hearts in hope that someone or something will come and restore us to wholeness. Sometimes the pain is overwhelming.

Jesus desperately wants to meet us in our darkest places, to enter into the space of our deepest hurt and hold us close. God became human in Jesus—*human*. God lovingly chose to take on our form, our very nature, so that we would no longer wander in hopelessness. The divine walks with us in our humanity so that our fragile existence will not devour us. Jesus takes our pain and embraces it. In the midst of what is sometimes a most frightening silence, Jesus calls us by name and brings us home to the love of God.

We do not have to stay in the dark places. We can find the healing necessary to stand, walk, and live in the protection of the Christ, the anointed one who provides a way through it all. Jesus is the shining light for us to follow through the shadows. There is no theological construct, doctrine, or thesis that can come close to the comfort and solace found when the voice of the risen Jesus gently calls out: "I love you. You are mine."

- How does it make us feel to know that we belong to Jesus?
- Who can we lean on to help us turn all of our fears, anxieties, and pain over to the love of Christ?
- What can we learn from experiences of sadness and grief?

Christ Jesus,
sometimes our despair
is so deep
and crippling
that we can barely move.
We need you so much
to help us break through
our grief and sadness.
Come, please,
and call us by name,
and help us to stand up,
walk, and live again.

Amen.

Chapter 6
resurrection:
rising to new Life in jesus

The way of Jesus is thus not
a set of beliefs about Jesus…
the way of Jesus is the way of death and resurrection -
the path of transition and transformation
from an old way of being to a new way of being.

—Marcus J. Borg

Jesus Christ and the gospel are not two separate things.
The gospel is not a biography of Christ.
For St. Paul, the gospel is the living power of God.
Reading the gospel is not like reading an ordinary book.
You have to fill yourself with faith
and stress the living Jesus Christ.

—Oscar Romero

Love is the person of the resurrection,
scooping up the dust and chanting, "live!"

—Emily Dickinson

Song of the Risen One

Disc 2 • Track 8

Why do you look for the liv-ing a-mong the dead?
He is not here: he has been raised to new
life! Al-le-lu-ia, al-le-lu-ia!

Come and see!
The one whom you seek is no longer here:
Who is risen among you,
who goes now before you, alive!
Alleluia! Alleluia!

Every tear
will be driven away; no more pain!
No more weeping and mourning,
behold, I make all things new!
Alleluia! Alleluia!

Strength to the weak!
New sight for the blind: Jesus alive!
Go and tell all the nations
the wondrous deeds of our God!
Alleluia! Alleluia!

Text: Based on Luke 24:5–6, Matthew 11:4–5, 28:6–7, 19, Revelation 7:17, 21:4–5; David Haas
Tune: David Haas
© 1988, GIA Publications, Inc.

Even when we desperately want to believe in something, when our prayers actually come true, we still can at times, feel suspicious. We want to believe with everything we have and are that good news is stronger than bad news, and that hope and promise actually do win out over despair and broken dreams.

Here it is true: the resurrection is real, and it is now. Our human condition understandably wants to look for a loophole, an explanation that will ratify our suspicion in a world where hope is shattered on a daily basis. But here it is true: the resurrection is real, and it is now.

Part of being "dead" is refusing the invitation to stand up and embrace the realities all around us, that there is still more good news to find than bad news. Being "alive" is looking deeper, not in the places of empty tombs, but in the beauty of a resurrected creation where conversion and transformation can be found in the obvious and all-too-often subtle occurrences of life and love.

When real and honest resurrection emerges, it is amazing, awesome, unbelievable, earth-shaking and, yes, even disruptive. Hopefully this disruptive experience will urge us to cease looking for life in places of death and provoke us to look in other places to find that tears do not last, our pain will not always cripple us, we will see again with new eyes, and the song of resurrection and hope will deafen the voices of despair and death. Alleluia!

- What are some of the realities in our lives that can lead to a sense of hopelessness, where no resurrection seems to be in sight?
- Where can we find hope that we, too, can rise again in the midst of everything?
- How can we be living and breathing signs of resurrection to others?

Christ Jesus,
over and over again
you break through our hopelessness.
You rise again and again
in the places of our lives
where all seems lost;
you rise again and again
in our hearts
when they seem all but totally broken.
Come now,
and continue to amaze us,
letting your resurrection
move and breathe within us,
and guide us to new hope.

Amen.

TABLE SONG

Disc 2 • Track 9

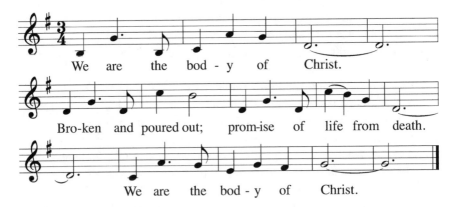

We are the bod-y of Christ.

Bro-ken and poured out; prom-ise of life from death.

We are the bod-y of Christ.

Is not the bread of life we break,
a sharing in the life of God?
Is not the cup of peace outpoured,
the blood of Christ?

How shall we make a return to God,
for goodness unsurpassing?
This saving cup we shall hold high,
and call out God's name!

Come taste and see the goodness,
the wonders of the Risen One!
Come bless our God in all things,
let praise be our song!

Text: Based on Psalms 116:12–13, 34:1, 8; 1 Corinthians 10:16; David Haas
Tune: David Haas
© 1991, GIA Publications, Inc.

We are the Body of Christ. The Paschal Mystery—the life, death and resurrection of Jesus—is passed on to us by the grace of God. Grace can be seen as the engine and power source of God's movement in our lives. Grace is given to all of us, shapes us as a community of believers, and names us as the people of God. So we, like the bread broken and wine poured at the Lord's altar, are the Body of Christ, offered to the world in ministry and service.

The simple actions of breaking and pouring at a singular table propel us to build many tables and engage ourselves in a daily sacrifice of being broken and poured out for each other. Our sharing in the real presence of Christ Jesus calls for a response from all of us to do more than consume the sacred meal. It is also an invitation to consume the presence of Christ that we experience in each other, and hopefully urges us to be consumed with becoming that presence to the world, fully and absolutely.

> We are the Body of Christ.
>> Our return to God is for us to behave as such.
> We are the Body of Christ.
>> We should hold high this sacred identity, without reserve, for the life of the world.
> We are the Body of Christ.
>> We should invite all to taste and see this experience.
> We are the Body of Christ.
>> We are called to become a blessing in all that we do, and all that we are.

> We need to say, believe, and live it, again and again: we are the Body of Christ.

- If we are the Body of Christ, for what are we consecrated and what are we sent to do?
- What does our experience of the Paschal Mystery teach us about who Jesus is?
- What are specific ways that we can help build up the Body in our lives, work, ministry, and relationships?

Christ Jesus,
we have seen you
and tasted your presence in our lives.
Come now
and help us to become your body,
your presence,
and your nourishment for the world.

Help us to embrace your brokenness
so that we, too, may be
broken and poured out
for all who seek you
and for all who seek life.

Amen.

CHRIST IS RISEN! SHOUT HOSANNA!

Disc 2 • Track 10

1. Christ is ris-en! Shout Ho - san-na! Cel - e-brate this
2. Christ is ris-en! Raise your spir-its from the cav-erns
3. Christ is ris-en! Earth and heav-en nev-er-more shall

day of days! Christ is ris - en! Hush in won-der:
of des - pair. Walk with glad-ness in the morn-ing,
be the same. Break the bread of new cre - a - tion

all cre - a - tion is a-mazed. In the des - ert
see what love can do and dare. Drink the wine of
where the world is still in pain. Tell its grim, de -

all - sur-round-ing, see, a spread-ing tree has grown.
res - ur - rec - tion, not a ser - vant, but a friend.
mon - ic, cho - rus: "Christ is ris - en! Get you gone!"

Heal-ing leaves of grace a - bound-ing bring a taste
Je - sus is our strong com - pan-ion, Joy and peace
God the first and last is with us. Sing Ho - san -

of love un - known.
shall nev - er end.
na ev - 'ry - one!

Text: Brian Wren; © 1986 Hope Publishing Company.
Tune: David Haas; © 1991, GIA Publications, Inc.

It is almost impossible to celebrate resurrection when everything around us seems to proclaim the opposite. It is a struggle beyond belief to enter into a song of rejoicing when all we see is selfishness, greed, addiction, hatred, racism, gossip, war, loneliness, and so many other manifestations of a world that seem to embody anything but the Reign of God. Yet we are called upon to celebrate.

Easter is not a celebration of the absence of what seems at times to be hell, but rather, one that proclaims loudly to such hell that it will not win. It will not have the last word. The signs of this are often subtle: we find them in the presence of a growing and spreading tree where the healing leaves of grace fall all around us, promising that all shall be well.

Easter does not deny the pain of the world, but stares in the face of all that would attempt to destroy us and says, "Get you gone!" Easter is the promise that God is with us. Easter is Jesus rising above the dryness of the desert, inviting us to drink the wine of resurrection that can become the medicine we need to survive and be healed from our caverns of despair. Easter helps us to walk with gladness even when the path is filled with detours and destruction that stall us temporarily.

When all seems lost, we still sing "Hosanna!" When we feel too tired to go on, we still sing "Hosanna!" When we feel that evil is stronger than our attempts for good, we still sing "Hosanna!" The Christ, the first and last, is with us. Sing "Hosanna!"

- What do we need to do so we do not miss the subtle signs of resurrection all around us?
- How can we clear our spiritual path to be more attentive to the many risings in store for us?
- In the midst of the many signs of despair along the way, where do we find the hope and belief needed to keep us afloat?

Christ Jesus,
we are called to sing
and rejoice in resurrection,
but there are so many signs
and realities that point elsewhere.
Come now
and help us see past these
blocks along the way

and recognize the many
and sometimes hidden truths
that remind us that you are here,
alive and risen,
now and always.

Amen.

Without Seeing You

Disc 2 • Track 11

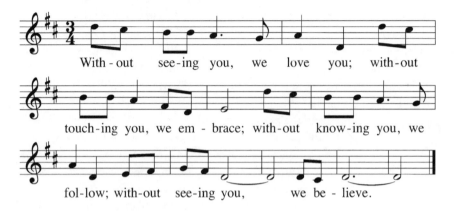

With-out   see-ing you,   we   love   you;   with-out   touch-ing you, we em - brace; with-out   know-ing you, we   fol-low; with-out   see-ing you,   we be - lieve.

We return to you deep within,
leave the past to the dust;
turn to you with tears and fasting;
you are ready to forgive.

The sparrow will find a home,
near to you, O God;
how happy, we who dwell with you,
forever in your house.

Text: Based on 1 Peter 1:8, Psalm 84; David Haas
Tune: David Haas
© 1993, GIA Publications, Inc.

To believe is a grave risk. Faith can seem to be a most irrational and flawed path to take in the complicated world where we live. Faith is a call to invest in something when most signs point us in a completely different direction.

To have faith in any human relationship is also accompanied by the painful truth that the other person is not perfect and that disappointment is all but inevitable. To have faith in Christ Jesus is to have faith in someone we cannot literally see or touch; someone who spent time with people many of us would never dare be seen with; someone who said and preached all kinds of things that make no sense at all ("love your enemies," "if you want to be first, you must be last"); and someone whose ultimate earthly destiny was death.

This person we cannot see tells us that he is the way, the truth and the life. How can we possibly put our faith in what seems to be a most feeble presence? We can if we stop looking for Jesus in the traditional way. When we feel the unconditional love and acceptance of a parent, a spouse, a close friend, we see Jesus. When we are the recipient of an embrace of forgiveness by another, we see Jesus. When we experience the grace of a community of love and care, we see Jesus. When we survive and grow from a painful experience or dreadful loss of some kind, we see Jesus.

When we are attentive to these things, belief can actually be very rational and visible. Our faith in Jesus is a gift, a presence so very real in so many ways, whether we see it or not.

- Where do we find the love and embrace of Christ in our life?
- How can we be more attentive to the presence of Jesus in prayer?
- How can we be living and breathing signs of resurrection to others?

Christ Jesus,
you ask each of us
to believe in you,
in your love for us,
and in your presence with us.
Come and strengthen our faith
to seek you out,
and to recognize your presence
in the many signs,
ordinary and extraordinary,
where you dwell.
Then we will really see you.

Amen.

Water of Life

Disc 2 ● Track 12

Wa-ter of life, Je-sus our light; jour-ney from death to new life. Wa-ter of life, Je-sus our light; jour-ney from death to new life.

Fountain of light, new sight for the blind,
we come to the water, we come now to see!

Fountain of compassion, freedom from fear,
we come to the water, we come to find peace!

Fountain of justice, free all our hate,
we come to the water, we come now to love!

Fountain of mercy, bind all our wounds,
we come to the water, we come to be healed!

Fountain of mission, calling our name,
we come to the water, we come now to serve!

Text: David Haas
Tune: David Haas
© 1987, GIA Publications, Inc.

Jesus has invited us to come to the waters of new life. He himself initiates his ministry at his own baptism; he heals the blind one at Siloam and rides through the storm with his friends, raising his hand to calm the raging torrents; he liberates and heals the Samaritan woman at the well and walks on water, over the abyss and tumult of the waters. On the cross water flows with blood from his side, and after the resurrection he sits alongside the water preparing the fish-fry for his disciples. What is it about Jesus and water?

Wherever there is water, things seem to happen. Water works in helping us understand Jesus because it moves and takes unpredictable turns. It is both calming and disruptive; it cleanses and can also destroy. Water brings about peace and solace, and also stirs things up in our lives. It is the path of what is often an unpredictable journey.

And so it is with our journey with Jesus. In the end, we believe that this journey brings us to life. The fountain of life is exactly that—a fountain that spurts up and around us, sometimes with great force, sometimes like a small trickle. But it keeps coming. Jesus keeps coming—moving toward us, asking us to join in the flow.

Our baptism is with water—not because it is stagnant, but because it moves, moistens, and nourishes. We may hit tough currents, but the water keeps moving, and when this journey settles, when we hopefully see Jesus face to face, new life is found, forever.

- What change does our baptism call us to make?
- What keeps us from joining in the flow with Jesus and his care for us?
- How can we recommit and reaffirm our baptismal call, right here, right now?

Christ Jesus,
you have baptized us
in the fountain of your love
and grace.
Through this grace
you have named us as your people.
Come and help us
to join the flow,

to move with the current,
with faith
that you will lead and guide us
and keep us safe
in the journey from death
to new life.

Amen.

Alive in Christ Jesus

Disc 2 • Track 13

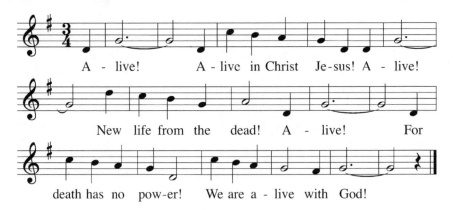

A - live!   A - live in Christ   Je-sus! A - live!

New   life from the   dead!   A - live!   For

death has no   pow-er!   We are a - live with   God!

Are you not aware?
We who were born in Christ Jesus
were born into his death!
Are you not aware?
We were buried with Jesus,
that we too might live!
Are you not aware?
We are united with him,
so that we will rise now with him!

This we know:
That our darkness has died,
we are slaves no longer!
This we know:
If we have died with Christ,
we too shall live!
This we know:
The Christ who has risen,
will never die!
This we know:
This death was death to sin,
once for all!

Text: Based on Romans 6:3–11; David Haas
Tune: David Haas
© 1991, GIA Publications, Inc.

What does it mean to be truly alive? We know many who move, breathe, walk around, go to work, and so on, but do not seem to be really "alive." "New life from the dead" is much more than a literal reference—"new life from the dead" means a major jump-start to our patterns and behaviors.

This text from Romans 6:3–11 challenges us to realize that our baptism and adoption as daughters and sons of God in the light of Christ has a twist. Remember that at baptism we are signed with the cross. In other words, we begin our new life in Christ under the symbol of an instrument of death.

To follow Jesus means we are also called to the cross with him. To follow Jesus, we, too, must die to many things. To follow Jesus means that we have to face our fears. But we do so knowing that Jesus, who walks with us every step of the way, promises life on the other side.

His historical death was not *literally* death to sin, once for all. We know that even after his historical death and resurrection sin still exists and pervades the universe. So what does it really mean? It means that while sin still surrounds us, it is no longer a force that will ultimately destroy us. This is what it is to be alive in Christ Jesus.

Death, sadness, pain, and all the other demons that haunt us no longer hold pride of place in our spiritual lives. Each time we say yes to this new life, the powers that usually hold us down are pulled away, and we are left with the blessed love of this Christ calls us by name and infuses us with his Spirit, making us fully alive!

- What is the real promise given to us by being born in Christ Jesus?
- How can we deepen the commitment to accept the burdens given to us as Christians symbolized each time we make the sign of the cross?
- What choices can we make to be more alive in our faith?

Christ Jesus,
you have stared death right in the eyes
and destroyed its power.
You have said "no more"
to the demons that surrounded
your life.
Come now and free us
from the many forces
that would do us harm.
Help us to be alive—
really alive—
in your light and presence.

Amen.

Do This in Memory of Me

Disc 2 ● Track 14

Take and eat, this is my bod - y.

Take and drink, this is my blood;

shared that you may be for - giv - en.

Do this in mem - 'ry of me.

Do this in mem - 'ry of me.

Christ has died, Christ is risen.
Christ will come, Christ will come again!

Dying you destroyed our death,
rising you restored our life.
Lord Jesus, come, Lord Jesus, come in glory!

When we eat this bread,
when we drink this cup,
we proclaim your death, until you come in glory!

Text: Based on Matthew 26:26–29; Mark 14:22–25; Luke 22:14–20; David Haas;
Excerpts from the English Translation of the Roman Missal
Copyright © 1973 International Committee on English in the Liturgy, Inc. (ICEL)
Tune: David Haas
© 2001, 2003, GIA Publications, Inc.

The words of this refrain articulate the greatest action of love and companionship that Jesus shows to his closest friends. The Eucharist is the ultimate lifeline for those of us who move forward in hope to find intimacy and communion with the Risen Lord. Jesus did not have to do this. The apostles and followers certainly did not earn any favors through their inconsistencies in faithfulness shown in those final days. But the gift was given—another tremendous grace from the unconditional life and love of Christ.

This holy meal, this great mystery of faith is our most profound theology and our most precious gift as we muddle through life. To sit at table and dine with Jesus is to feast upon the most-loving presence of thankfulness, joy, mercy, compassion, justice, and peace. Jesus is all of these things, and all of these things are made new, possible, vibrant, and passionate because of him. When Jesus says to "do this," we are challenged to be ministers and messengers of all that we are called to be and proclaim. We do more than share in a sacred meal, as blessed as it is. We are called to live and call forth the Reign of God. That is the "this" of "do this."

- What are the ways in which the celebration of the Eucharist shapes our choices, ministry, and lives?
- "Do this in memory of me." How can we best proclaim this memory of Jesus?
- How are we honoring the presence of Christ at the many tables where we sit?

Christ Jesus,
you have done a most blessed thing
in your inviting us
to share in your presence
every time we gather
in your name.
Stay close to us,
keep your presence ever alive
and ever moving
in our lives,
in our choices,
in our work,
in our relationships,
and most of all,
when we celebrate
and give praise to you.

Amen.

Here in This Place

Disc 2 • Track 15

Are not our hearts burn - ing with - in us?

Are not our lives shared as one bread?

Here in our hands, here in this place.

Je - sus, our hope; life from the dead.

In the breaking of the bread,
you are all we need.
We were lost, and now are found;
home again with God.

You are food for all our hunger;
you are all we need.
You are our promise and our hope,
life for the world.

As this bread is broken,
as this cup is shared,
we give our lives: broken and outpoured.
We will serve the Lord.

Text: Based on Luke 24:13–15; David Haas
Tune: David Haas
© 1988, GIA Publications, Inc.

Passion, whether we are conscious about it or not, is a common desire for all who long to have their faith strengthened. We are often attracted to and to respond to those who are passionate about their vocation, interests, beliefs, and convictions. We need to hear, sing, and dance the many stories that give testimony to a pilgrim people who are strong in their faith.

This story is typical of many we find in the Gospels in which those searching for meaning and hope encounter Jesus. He stirs up their emotions, but more than that, he enlivens their desire for transformation and reconciliation.

When Jesus enters our heart—and when we accept his presence—we are given new energy. We too, rise again. We experience a new way of seeing and treating each other as agents of forgiveness and compassion. We receive a fresh approach in how we live, doing so with passionate care and resolve. We are filled to the brim with Jesus, the living Word of God.

We share in the breaking of the bread, but also in the true communion of solidarity with each other. We are no longer lost, but found in the sharing of Word and meal. When this happens, the natural response is service. When our hearts burn with the presence and knowledge of Christ Jesus, here in this place, hope, life, and kingdom can be recognized and realized.

- What are our passions, the things that burn in our hearts?
- When we listen to the voice of Jesus, what are we being asked to do?
- How can we use our passionate faith to bring hope to others?

Christ Jesus,
when we hear your voice
our hearts burn with passion.
When we feel your presence
our lives are alive with purpose.
Come now,
here in this time and place,
and be our hope,
be new life for all of us
who feel dead,
who long for new breath,
new life,
and new promises.
Help us to spin our passion
into service for your people.

Amen.

The Tomb Is Empty

Disc 2 • Track 16

1. The tomb is emp - ty, is emp-ty!
2. The tomb is emp - ty, is emp-ty!
3. The tomb is emp - ty, is emp-ty!
4. The tomb is emp - ty, is emp-ty!
5. The tomb is emp - ty, is emp-ty!

Come and see where once the
Come and hear these words of
Come and touch the stone and
Come and meet the ris - en
Go and serve all peo - ple who

bod - y lay. Can it be
life and peace: "He is not
fold - ed shroud. Christ lives in -
Christ our Lord in whom we
long to be free! Raise those who

true, be true that Je - sus Christ
here, not here. He lives a - gain
deed, in - deed. Al - le - lu - ia!
have, we have our vic - to - ry,
sleep, who sleep in tombs of fear,

is raised to life to - day?
in all your Ga - li - lees."
Be - liev - ers, shout a - loud.
in whom is life re - stored.
and give them eyes to see!

Sing al - le-lu - ia! Sing al - le -

lu - ia!

Text: Sts. 1–4, Sylvia G. Dunstan, St. 5, David Haas
Tune: David Haas
© 1991, 2003, GIA Publications, Inc.

Tombs do not exist only in cemeteries; they are also found in the deepest places of our hearts. These tombs hold our sadness, sin, despair, and shame.

Too many of us are kept poisoned and trapped in tombs of self-hatred and imprisoned in tombs of loneliness, addiction, and sickness. Too many of us are confined in tombs of abuse and violence, bound by chains of racism, discrimination, and hatred.

Jesus comes into our lives and proclaims that this does not have to be the way. He holds our shame close to his loving heart, knowing our darkest places and providing healing and acceptance. Jesus brings companionship and friendship, and helps us find a path unobstructed by the forces and substances we use to medicate our pain and suffering.

Jesus showers us with love that washes away the horrors that haunt us, breaks down all barriers, and calls every person to become a child of God.

If we want, we can be freed from our tombs if we say yes to Jesus. We can rejoice in the truth of the resurrection. We can find true victory in which our lives are restored and fear is calmed by the power of the love of Christ, risen forever.

- What are the forces and demons that lock us in our tombs?
- What words of Christ Jesus give us hope in the possibility of new life?
- Who are our brothers and sisters presently living imprisoned in tombs of fear?
- How can we help bring the love of Jesus to their pain?

Christ Jesus,
you are the resurrected one,
the one who has conquered
the tomb of darkness and death.
Come now,
hear our cries of despair
and help free us from the many prisons
that we find ourselves in
and have created ourselves.
Come now
and roll the stones away
from all that keeps us
from rising to new life in you.
Come now
and rise again in us.

Amen.

Chapter 7

mission:
our call in the name of jesus

The Risen Christ is with us today,
and he continues to need each one of you.
Jesus needs your eyes to continue to see.
He needs your strength to continue to work.
He needs your voice to continue to teach.
He needs your hands to continue to bless.
He needs your heart to continue to love.
And Jesus needs your whole being
to continue to build his body, the Church.
As we believe, so let us live!

—*Joseph Bernardin*

Indeed, to live a spiritual life
means to become living Christs.
It is not enough to try to imitate Christ
as much as possible;
it is not enough to
remind others of Jesus;
it is not even enough to be inspired
by the words and actions of Jesus Christ.
No, the spiritual life presents us
with a far more radical demand:
to be living Christs here and now,
in time and history.

—*Henri J. M. Nouwen*

Christianity discerns that beyond the night
the dawn already glows.
The hope that does not fail is carried in the heart.
Christ goes with us!

—*Oscar Romero*

Now We Remain

Disc 2 • Track 17

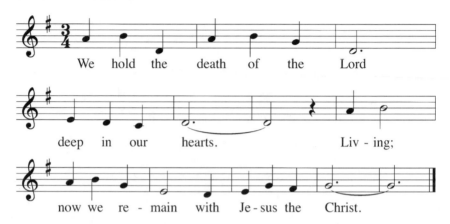

Once we were people afraid, lost in the night.
Then by your cross we were saved;
dead became living, life from your giving.

Something which we have known,
something we've touched,
what we have seen with our eyes:
This we have heard, life-giving Word.

He chose to give of himself, became our bread.
Broken, that we might live.
Love beyond love, pain for our pain.

We are the presence of God: this is our call.
Now to become bread and wine:
food for the hungry, life for the weary,
for to live with the Lord, we must die with the Lord!

Text: Based on 1 Peter 8, 1 John 1:1–3, 2 Timothy 2:11; David Haas
Tune: David Haas
© 1983, GIA Publications, Inc.

Nothing good or fulfilling comes without some cost. For the early followers, saints, and heroes who followed the promise of Jesus, the cost was significant. For some, embracing the way of Christ meant isolation; for many more it meant death. Here again is the paradox of Jesus and his ministry.

While we are not masochistic, as Christians we do not run from death. We embrace it as part and parcel of the mystery of Christ. We hold the death of the Lord deep in our hearts. By doing so we are connected intimately with Jesus, and all that invites sadness and death is conquered by the one who loves us beyond our imagination.

To walk this walk is to share in his mission. Together with Jesus, we are caught up in God's cause to be food for the hungry and life for those too weary to hope. We are here, the presence of God, dying and living with Christ so that this gift may be at the center of our life and mission.

Jesus was not a puppet on God's string; he chose to give of himself so completely because he was fully in love with God. The love shown through the tremendous self-giving of Jesus is the love we are asked to lavish upon each other—those we love and especially those we find it difficult to love. There are no distinctions in Christ's love for us, and neither are there distinctions as to whom we are to serve in the name of Jesus. Now we remain with Jesus; to do so means to live and die with him.

- What does it cost us to follow Jesus more faithfully?
- How can we nurture our spiritual lives to grow in our relationship with Christ?
- Can we make more room in our hearts to carry the suffering of Christ?

Christ Jesus,
we stumble throughout our lives,
hoping and groping for meaning.
In you, in your suffering
we find a way to live
for the sake of others.
Come to us
and instill in us your spirit
of self-giving,

of sacrifice,
of unconditional love,
and we will know
what it means to follow you
and remain with you
in the protection of your love.

Amen.

Be Light for Our Eyes

Disc 2 ● Track 18

Come and be light for our eyes; be the air we breathe, be the voice we speak! Come, be the song we sing, be the path we seek!

Your life was given, food for all people;
body and blood, new life in our midst!
Death is no longer; life is our future.
Jesus, Messiah: name of all names!

We hold your presence, risen forever!
Your name now names us: People of God!
Filled with your vision, people of mission;
healing, forgiving; light for the world!

Lead us to justice, light in the darkness;
singing, proclaiming Jesus is Lord!
Teach us to speak, and help us to listen
for when your truth and our dreams embrace!

Text: David Haas
Tune: David Haas
© 1985, GIA Publications, Inc.

To put on Christ, to allow Jesus to guide and inform every part of our lives, requires total surrender and an openness to be taken over. To let go of control is a painfully difficult yet necessary grounding for our discipleship. It is so hard to release our mind, heart, and will to a power greater than ourselves. Those in various types of recovery from their addictions have a lot to teach us in this regard. Such surrender means more than mere survival. It becomes the genesis of new life, new healing, and new energy and vision.

When we ascribe to the vision of God, when we let the risen Lord take us over to become our eyes, breath, and voice, we are able to see and speak with much greater clarity and fidelity to God's cause. When we get out of the way and let Christ reign in our service we see the reversal of expectations and assumptions that block our ability to be partners in building God's kingdom.

When we release our ego and let the way of Jesus guide our choices we become more focused, more faithful. When we let our pride melt away we listen more attentively and are more receptive to Jesus being Lord of our lives.

This is the song we need to sing over and over again: the song of surrender, of unceasing rejoicing that God has chosen us to be ambassadors for Christ and his Gospel.

- What gets in the way of allowing the light of Christ to guide our lives?
- Jesus is calling us to share in his mission. What might that look like for us in concrete terms?
- How can we listen and live more intently in the way of Jesus?

Christ Jesus,
come now
and be light for our eyes.
Come and breathe your Spirit
deep within us
and help us now
to sing your song of Good News.
We hold your presence
close to us,
for we are your people.
We call out to you
to lead us,
to guide us,
to become your words,
your hands,
and your heart to the world.

Amen.

Christ among Us

Disc 2 • Track 19

1. Christ has no bod-y now on earth but ours:
2. Christ has no voice now on earth but ours:
3. Christ has no heart now on earth but ours:
4. Christ has no light now on earth but ours:

Our hands are to be his hands, our feet are to
Our thoughts are to be his thoughts, our words are to
Our touch is to be his touch, our care is to
Our hope is to be his hope, our strength is to

be his feet, our eyes are now his eyes.
be his words, our song is now his song.
be his care, our love is now his love.
be his strength, our joy is now his joy.

Christ has no bod-y now on earth but ours.
Christ has no voice now on earth but ours.
Christ has no heart now on earth but ours.
Christ has no light now on earth but ours.

Text: Based on a prayer of St. Therese of Avila, 1515–1582; David Haas
Tune: David Haas
© 2007, GIA Publications, Inc.

Believe it or not, Jesus does not accomplish and bring forth the Reign of God all on his own. We must play a part as well. Under no uncertain terms we are called to be the presence of Christ in all that we do, to all we meet, and in the midst of our choices and decisions.

To be a disciple of Jesus Christ is more than merely assenting to his teachings and participating in praise and worship. The gift of Jesus demands a total life response through the power of the Holy Spirit. What does that mean concretely?

It means that as Jesus healed the sick, we, too, are called to bring the compassion and healing message of Jesus to all those in need—physically, mentally, and spiritually. It means that as Jesus brought the precious gifts of forgiveness and mercy to the many sinners that he encountered, we, too, are to be model witnesses of that same mercy to those desperately in need of God's unconditional love. It means that as Jesus was an agent for conversion and repentance, we, too, are to sing and proclaim the marvelous gift of transformation that is available to all who would follow.

We are to be the living, breathing, walking, and passionate presence of Jesus—to be his hands, voice, and heart, and to radiate his light to all we encounter and seek out. There is no mysterious, magical, mystical, or paranormal strategy to announce and make real God's reign. We, the ordinary and yet, at the same time, blessed daughters and sons of God are the ones called to make this Jesus known, loved, and followed.

- If we are to be this presence of Christ to the world, where do we begin?
- How can we help influence this presence in our work, at our parish or school, and in our families and relationships with others?
- Where do we receive the strength needed to respond to Jesus' call to serve so completely?

Christ Jesus,
you call us to take on
a very daunting task.
We are afraid of your call
to be your presence,
your voice,
and your mind and heart.
Help us to "get over" ourselves
and be open to receive
the strength and wisdom we need
to be your servants
and your light to the world.

Amen.

You Are God's Work of Art

Disc 2 • Track 20

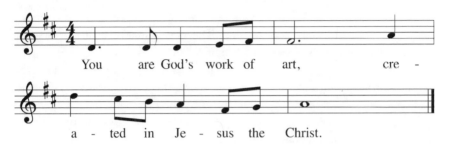

You are God's work of art, cre-a-ted in Je-sus the Christ.

You have been enlightened by the Lord;
Walk as children of the light.

Keep the flame of faith in your heart,
and may you meet him when he comes.

Blessed be our God,
who chose you in the light of Christ.

Text: Based on Ephesians 2:10 and The Rite of Baptism; David Haas
Tune: David Haas
© 1988, GIA Publications, Inc.

What a wonderful and precious image for us! We are God's work of art. God sees us as art, and good art is concerned with beauty, inspiration, depth, symbolism, communication, and all that is noble and worthy. God's *perfect* work of art is Jesus: teacher, healer, reconciler, savior, messiah, lover, troublemaker, agitator, caregiver, companion, hope, compassion, mercy... no litany can contain the depth of the gift of Christ proclaimed and known by us who follow, hopefully with the flame of faith in our hearts.

Our baptism claims us as God's work of art, an extension, expression, and celebration of Jesus to be light for the world. It sounds lofty, and it is. God calls and names us at the get-go as a work of art, then gives us Jesus as the standard. We are chosen to be the light of Christ. What does that mean? It does not mean that we follow a recipe approach to being the presence of Jesus (i.e., what would Jesus do?), but rather challenges us to examine, reflect, and push ourselves to get inside the deeper story of the mission and endpoint for a life lived in the radiance of Christ.

We cannot begin to imitate to perfection the witness of the historical Jesus, but we can attempt to clothe ourselves with the greater charge to speak, act, and live in the name of the risen Christ—to preach, live, and sing resurrection with every bit of passion that we have.

- What are the gifts of beauty and art that Jesus sees in us?
- Where do we see signs of the risen Christ in our everyday life?
- To what mission have we been specifically chosen to live as followers of Jesus?

Christ Jesus,
you are the light that guides us,
the fire that burns in our hearts,
and our brother for the journey.
Come to us in our darkness
and shine with the blaze
of new faith and new possibilities.
We bless you and thank you
for walking with us
as we together
bring your name and presence
to a world aching for hope.

Amen.

For the Life of the World

Disc 2 • Track 21

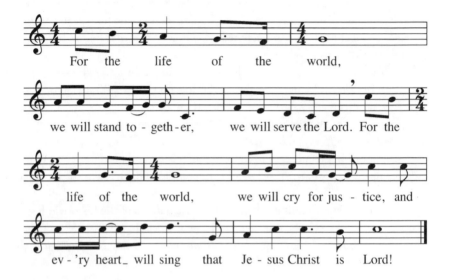

We walk together to be children of light,
our God calls each of us by name!
Christ moves within us, we are God's work of art!
We live no longer for ourselves!

We are empowered by the love of Christ,
whose life has conquered sin and death!
There is no other name but Jesus the Lord!
We live no longer for ourselves!

We are the chosen people God has called,
the life we live is not our own!
If we will die with Christ, then we will be free!
We live no longer for ourselves!

The lost and broken will be healed from their shame,
the poor will see the face of God!
Sent by the Spirit, we are called to serve!
We live no longer for ourselves!

Text: David Haas
Tune: David Haas

In our desire to be more faithful, focused, and committed in our life in Christ we sometimes forget to ask ourselves *why*. Why is Jesus important? Why is our vocation to serve and witness to the light of Christ worthwhile? Why do we do all this?

We do so for the life of the world. All our effort, energy, drive, and time to seek to know Jesus more intensely is for the life of the world. And we are called to do this in the solidarity of community, not isolated in our own spiritual box. We walk together; we are God's people. We are called by name, together, as God's great work of art. We are the chosen people of God, chosen to sing and proclaim Jesus as Lord. We are called to collectively present the face of God through the saving mission of Christ. Not alone, but together we are sent forth into the world to serve and to die with Christ—to suffer and offer our lives to be broken—so that freedom is not just a concept, but a living, breathing reality of what the Good News promises.

We live no longer for ourselves. We live and die for each other, and we do so in solidarity with each other. We stand together. We serve together, with and for Christ. The life of the world depends on it.

- How can we be more receptive in allowing the light of Christ to shine in our life?
- Where do we find a community of love and support to live for the life of the world?
- What specifically can we do to be more faithful in our discipleship?

Christ Jesus,
you are the light
that shines deeply in our lives.
You are the love of God
made human and real,
given freely to us.
You call us chosen
to help bring your reign to birth.
You are the face of God.
Come now
and infuse in us
the light and energy necessary
to live no longer for ourselves
but for the life of your people.

Amen.

Jesus, Be with Us Now

Disc 2 • Track 22

Broken, your people, we who are your own.
Mend us in the shape of your love, formed in you.

Scattered and fractured, frozen in our fear.
Bind us, unite us as one, strangers no more.

With singing and in silence, we come with open hands.
In blessing, in breaking the bread, we become you.

Text: David Haas
Tune: David Haas
© 1997, GIA Publications, Inc.

All that we are, all that we have been given, all that we hope to be—we strive to give all we have to Christ for the life of others. Jesus calls us all to be instruments for Good News—for healing, blessing, and new life.

We believe that Jesus was broken and poured out as a sign to the world that his love for us is complete, unconditional, and without reserve. We have been given the call to be this same sign to the world. Our fears as well as our gifts are partnered together to proclaim Jesus crucified and risen. We live in a time and world that is fractured and torn apart, and so the mission becomes more urgent to take, bless, break, and give: to give of our very selves for each other, our sisters and brothers in the Lord.

It is through the sacred meal of the Eucharist that we come face to face with the gift that is given so lavishly for us—Jesus, the Christ, the anointed one, our song of justice and peace. We long to be united in this relationship, and we call upon Jesus to be with us. Now.

- In what ways can we commit ourselves more intentionally to be signs of Jesus' presence?
- What are the signs around us that proclaim this presence loudly and clearly?
- How can we turn our brokenness and the work of our hands into blessings for the world?

Christ Jesus,
all we are
and all we have
belongs to you.
Call each of us,
right here, right now,
to be your sign, your blessing,
your gift of new life.
With your strength
there is nothing that we cannot do
to bring all closer to you.
Come now,
right here, right now,
and be with us.

Amen.

Give Me Jesus

Disc 2 • Track 23

Oh, when I am alone, Oh, when I am alone,
Oh, when I am alone, give me Jesus.

Give me Je - sus, give me
Je - sus, you may have all this
world, give me Je - sus.

Dark midnight was my cry, dark midnight was my cry;
dark midnight was my cry, give me Jesus.

Oh, when I come to die, Oh, when I come to die,
Oh, when I come to die, give me Jesus.

Oh, when I want to sing, Oh, when I want to sing,
Oh, when I want to sing, give me Jesus.

Text: Traditional African-American spiritual
Tune: Traditional African-American spiritual; arr. David Haas

The old African-American spirituals are precious gifts, the result of the Paschal Mystery being played out in the narrative of a most horrific yet redemptive story of slavery and oppression. These songs were and still are more than songs of comfort for the slave. These expressions are the very voice of faith and survival.

These songs of lament and hope put real skin on the terror of life and offer a way of transformation and healing. They cut to the quick and lay out the path for us to rise above all our ills, questions, anxieties, and dashed hopes. Here the slave is our teacher and guide, showing us who Jesus is. Theologians, as important as they are, sometimes make the case too difficult, too complex, filled with jargon and heady concepts. In the fields of oppressive violence and abuse, the theology proclaimed by the slave is far from being watered down. Rather, it is corrective.

Give me Jesus.
When I feel so tired and broken down, and feel as if I cannot continue—
    Give me Jesus.
When I experience such a sense of loneliness that tears become my food
        and drink—
    Give me Jesus.
When my sadness and fear paralyze every inch of my soul—
    Give me Jesus.
When I cannot find any reason to choose life in the midst of such
        paralyzing depression—
    Give me Jesus.

And when I feel the pure joy that comes from knowing that I am not alone on the journey, what song do I sing? *Give me Jesus.*

- When we are in our own dark midnight, for what or whom do we call out?
- Who can help us to draw upon the presence of Jesus in the worst of times?
- What songs help us feel close to Jesus and offer hope?

Christ Jesus,
when we are alone and fearful,
come and be close to us.
When we are sad beyond sad,
come and dry our tears.
When we find it difficult or impossible
    to go on,
come, hold our hands and hearts
and help us through the maze.

When we feel that no one feels or
    understands our pain,
come and make yourself known.
When we feel numb, disconnected, and
    deep in the quicksand,
pull us out, clean us up, and give us
    new strength to walk.
Come, Lord Jesus.

Amen.

Biblical Index

Liturgical Index

Holy Thursday

Good Friday

Easter

Ritual Index

About the Music

All of the music contained in this resource is published and available as individual choral editions from GIA Publications.

Choral Editions

Table Song G-3694
Take Up Your Cross G-5667
That You Might Have Life G-3449
The Encounter G-5219
The Tomb Is Empty G-6158
The Water I Give G-4866
To Be a Servant G-5185
Water of Life G-3496
We Are One in the Lord G-4747
We Have Been Told G-2662
Without Seeing You G-3928
You Alone Are the Word G-4867
You Are God's Work of Art G-4865
You Are Mine G-3656

Other Recorded and Published Music Collections by David Haas

Title	Collection	CD
A Time to Pray: For Justice and Peace	G-6868	CD-676
A Time to Pray: With the New Testament	G-6654	CD-643
A Time to Pray: With the Old Testament	G-6722	CD-644
As Water to the Thirsty	G-3062	CD-177
Before I Was Born	G-5180	CD-448
Biblical Way of the Cross	G-6615	CD-692
Blest Are They: The Best of David Haas, Vol. 1		CD-340
Come and Journey: David Haas, Marty Haugen, and Michael Joncas in Concert		CD-171
Creating God	G-3333	CD-213
Do This in Memory of Me: Holy Communion	G-5659	CD-554
Echo of Faith	G-5656	CD-507
Glory Day: David Haas and Friends in Concert	G-4849	CD-390
Glory to God: The Best of David Haas, Vol. 4		CD-806
God Has Done Marvelous Things (with Leon Roberts)	G-4731	
God Is Here	G-6687	CD-631
I Shall See God	G-3386	CD-226
Increase Our Faith: Parish Prayer Services for Whole Community Catechesis, Year B	G-6815	CD-664

Title	Collection	CD
Increase Our Faith: Parish Prayer Services		
for Whole Community Catechesis, Year C	G-6942	CD-695
Jesus, the Compassion of God	G-4990	
Light and Peace: Morning Praise		
and Evensong	G-3079	CD-175
Living Spirit, Holy Fire, Vol. 1		CD-716
Living Spirit, Holy Fire, Vol. 2		CD-731
Mass for the Life of the World	G-3889	CD-285
Mass of Light	G-3341	
No Longer Strangers	G-3946	CD-298
Psalms for the Church Year, Vol. 1		
(with Marty Haugen)	G-2664	CD-167
Psalms for the Church Year, Vol. 3		
(with Jeanne Cotter)	G-3325	CD-212
Psalms for the Church Year, Vol. 8	G-4579	CD-387
Psalms for the Church Year, Vol. 9	G-5041	CD-430
Reach toward Heaven	G-6161	CD-566
Singing Assembly: David Haas, Marty Haugen,		
and Michael Joncas in Concert		CD-209
Star Child: Music for Advent and Christmas	G-5206	CD-471
Table Songs: Music for Communion, Vol. 1	G-3694	CD-265
Table Songs: Music for Communion, Vol. 2	G-6450	CD-607
Throughout All Time	G-4713	CD-392
To Be Your Bread	G-2887	CD-172
Walking by Faith	G-4831	CD-412
We Give You Thanks	G-4989	CD-436
We Have Been Told	G-2700	CD-166
When Love Is Found: Music for Weddings	G-3745	G-3745CD
Where the River Flows	G-4335	CD-349
Who Calls You by Name:		
Music for Christian Initiation, Vol. 1	G-3193	CD-195
Who Calls You by Name:		
Music for Christian Initiation, Vol. 2	G-3622	CD-257
Winter Grace (with Jeanne Cotter)	G-3371	CD-206
With You by My Side, Vol. 1:		
The Journey of Life	G-5785	CD-517
With You by My Side, Vol. 2: Confirmation	G-5786	CD-518
Without Seeing You:		
The Best of David Haas, Vol. 3		CD-805

TITLE	COLLECTION	CD
You Are Mine: The Best of David Haas, Vol. 2		CD-341

References

The quotes by Oscar Romero are from *The Violence of Love: The Pastoral Wisdom of Archbishop Oscar Romero*, San Francisco: Harper and Row, 1988.

The quotes by Henri Nouwen are from *The Selfless Way of Christ: Downward Mobility and the Spiritual Life*, New York: Orbis Books, 2007, and *Letters to Marc About Jesus: Living the Spiritual Life in a Material World*, San Francisco: Harper, 1988.

The quotes by Richard Rohr are from *Everything Belongs: The Gift of Contemplative Prayer*, New York: The Crossroad Publishing Company, 1999, 2003.

The quote by Daniel Vestal is from *Being the Presence of Christ: A Vision for Transformation*, Nashville: Upper Room Books, 2008.

The quote from the United States Conference of Catholic Bishops is from *The National Directory for Catechesis*, Washington DC: United States Conference of Catholic Bishops, 2005.

The quote by Marcus Borg is from *Reading the Bible Again for the First Time: Taking the Bible Seriously but Not Literally*, San Francisco: Harper, 2001.

The quote by Joseph Bernardin is from *The Gift of Peace: Personal Reflections*, Chicago: Loyola Press, 1977.

About the Author

David Haas is the Director of The Emmaus Center for Music, Prayer, and Ministry and serves as Campus Minister and Artist-in-Residence at Benilde-St. Margaret's High School in St. Louis Park, Minnesota. Well known as one of the preeminent liturgical composers in the English-speaking world, he has recorded and published more than forty-five collections of original liturgical music and has written more than twenty books on the topics of music, liturgy, religious education, youth ministry, prayer, and spirituality.

He has traveled throughout the United States, Canada, the British Isles, Ireland, Europe, Australia, Israel, Greece, and Turkey as a conference and workshop speaker, concert performer, retreat leader, and recording artist, and was nominated for a Grammy Award in 1991 for the recording *I Shall See God* (GIA Publications). He is a regular columnist for *Ministry and Liturgy* magazine and the founder and executive director of *Music Ministry Alive!* (www.musicministryalive.com), a national liturgical music formation program for high school and college-aged youth.